Also by Piven & Cloward

REGULATING THE POOR

THE POLITICS OF TURMOIL

POOR PEOPLE'S MOVEMENTS

THE NEW
CLASS
WAR

Reagan's Attack

on the

Welfare State

and Its

Consequences

Pantheon Books
New York

THE NEW CLASS WAR

Frances Fox Piven
& Richard A. Cloward

Library of Congress Cataloging in Publication Data

Piven, Frances Fox.
The new class war.

Bibliography: p.
Includes index.
1. United States—Social policy—1980–
2. United States—Economic policy—1971–
3. Welfare state. 4. Social classes—United States.
I. Cloward, Richard A. II. Title.
HN59.2.P56   361.6'1'0973   81–48233
ISBN 0–394–52318–0   AACR2
ISBN 0–394–70647–1 (pbk.)

Grateful acknowledgment is made to the following for permission to reprint previously published material:

Daedalus: Excerpts from "Re-establishing an Economic Consensus: An Impossible Agenda?" by Barry Bosworth. Reprinted by permission of *Daedalus, Journal of the American Academy of Arts and Sciences* 109, no. 3 (summer 1980), Boston, Mass.

The Nation: Excerpt from "Forming a Real Women's Bloc" by Bella Abzug, November 28, 1981. Copyright © 1981 by Nation Magazine, The Nation Associates, Inc. Reprinted by permission.

The New York Times: Excerpt from *The New York Times*, November 10, 1981, D2. Copyright © 1981 by The New York Times Company. Reprinted by permission.

Contents

Acknowledgments

We want to thank our friends and colleagues who read and commented on this manuscript at various stages of its preparation: Robert Alford, Steve Becker, Henry Freedman, Albert Fried, Roger Friedland, David Gilman, Mitchell Ginsberg, Norman Glickman, Frances Goldin, Murray Levin, Harry Magdoff, Irving Miller, S. M. Miller, Paul Osterman, Barbara Rios, André Schiffrin, Lee Staples, John Tirman, Palmer Weber, Paul Wellstone, and Howard Zinn. As they will see, we incorporated most of their suggestions, although we took the risk of omitting some of them.

Barbara Williams and Hope Binham of the Columbia University School of Social Work staff were very helpful, as always, and we are grateful to them.

Introduction

*T*HE EMERGENCE OF the welfare state was a momentous development in American history. It meant that people could turn to government to shield them from the insecurities and hardships of an unrestrained market economy. One purpose of this essay is to explain why the business-oriented leaders who came to power with the election of Reagan in 1980 are trying to dismantle these protections.

Our other purpose is to say why we think they are likely to fail. This is not the first time men of property have combined to strip away the state programs on which the unemployed, the unemployable, and the working poor depend for their subsistence. However, if our conclusion turns out to be correct, it will be the first time the propertied meet defeat. Despite temporary setbacks, they have always managed in the past to eliminate whatever sources of subsistence were, from time to time, provided by the state. If the present-day corporate mobilization fails, that will be as significant as the emergence of the welfare state itself. It will mean that the developments in American society which brought the welfare state into being are also sufficient to ensure its persistence.

This conclusion is not implicit in our past writings on the relationships between the state, labor markets, and public relief. In *Regulating the Poor,* we examined those occasional and transient periods during which political protest provoked by mass unemployment sometimes forced governments to provide relief. Then, as disorder subsided, relief was cut back, thus restoring the economic insecurity that has been the driving force in the operation of labor markets.

Contemporary developments in American public relief seem to confirm this cyclical pattern. Once the protest movement of the 1960s waned, real benefit levels began to fall, as state legislatures refused to raise grant levels despite rapid inflation. Nor have the numbers receiving relief increased in response to the recessionary unemployment levels that have prevailed since the early 1970s. And the Reagan assault appears to be an effort to complete the restrictive phase of the relief cycle.

On the other hand, the great expansion of other social welfare programs which were initiated in either the 1930s or the 1960s was not aborted with the ebbing of protests in the 1970s. Relief recipients benefit enormously from some of these programs, especially those providing subsidies for food, fuel, and medical care, so that their condition has not worsened on the whole. Public relief, once the sole form of state intervention to ameliorate destitution, has thus come to be embedded in a general structure of income support programs for a wide range of constituencies, from the aged to the disabled to the unemployed. The changes in American society that gave rise to this development lead us to the conclusion that the cyclical pattern of providing subsistence resources by the state has been replaced by a variety of permanent income-maintenance entitlements.

We do not underestimate the scale and force of the contemporary corporate mobilization against the entitlement programs. Nevertheless, we think many different groups will join in resisting, and that this time they will prevail. The political economy of the late twentieth century is not that of either the eighteenth or the nineteenth century. The relationship of state to economy has been drastically altered in ways that provide powerful support for the idea that people have a right to subsistence, and particular legislative or executive actions will not extinguish that idea. We believe, in short, that *Regulating the Poor* represents a better characterization of the past than a prediction of the future, and it is the grounds for that belief which we explore in this book.

Much of what follows is necessarily historical. But it is history examined for the purpose of illuminating the present, and especially for the purpose of forecasting the outcome of the current struggle over the welfare state. If the political economy of the past several centuries prevented people from retaining the subsistence rights they had sometimes won, it is necessary to explain why, in the contemporary political economy, it is much less likely that they will lose again.

FRANCES FOX PIVEN
RICHARD A. CLOWARD
November 1981

I

CAPITALISM
AGAINST
DEMOCRACY

*I*N THE AFTERMATH of the election of 1980, the Reagan administration and its big-business allies declared a new class war on the unemployed, the unemployable, and the working poor. By the summer of 1981, congressional approval had been obtained to slash $140 billion from the social programs over the years 1982–1984, more than half of it from the income-maintenance programs that provide low-income people with cash, food, health care, and low-cost housing. At the same time, the Reagan administration announced that additional social program reductions of $45 billion and $30 billion would be proposed in 1983 and 1984, respectively, in order to achieve a balanced budget in 1984.

The attack on the income-maintenance programs of the

American social welfare state is indisputably a serious effort to reverse a pattern of government policy that has developed by fits and starts since the Great Depression. The attack has been direct and uncompromising, as shown by the Reagan administration's singlemindedness in pressing particular income-maintenance cuts on a Congress that accepted the overall argument for budgetary restraint but tried to moderate the impact on the poor by spreading the cuts over a wider range of budget categories, such as agricultural subsidies and the military budget.

Various justifications have been given for slashing the programs that provide a national income floor. One is that the voters themselves in the 1980 election showed they wanted the social programs to be cut. There is little evidence in support of this contention. Post-election opinion poll data indicate that the election was determined by concerns over concrete economic troubles and by vague anxieties over America's loss of leadership and respect in the world community. Carter was blamed for these ills, and it was the protest against his policies that turned the election to Reagan.

Of the various grounds for voter protest against the incumbent president, none was more important than the perception that the economy had been mismanaged. In the closing days of the campaign, and at a time of persisting high unemployment and unprecedented inflation, Reagan pointedly urged the American people to ask whether they had become better or worse off during the Carter presidency. And that scathing query was accompanied by a dramatic promise to turn the economy around. The post-election polls showed that enough voters were goaded by the question and persuaded by the promise to bring Reagan to the presidency. "It has never before happened in modern times," Walter Dean Burnham has since commented, "that the Republicans have been able to take the offensive on bread-and-butter issues" (p. 110). Moreover, it was unemployment rather than inflation that turned out to be the crucial issue in deciding the election. In both relative and absolute terms, the defections from Carter "were concentrated among those for whom unemployment was the most important problem. Among those selecting inflation, Reagan won by 67 percent, up only two points from Ford's 65 percent showing in 1976." By contrast, "among those worried about unemployment, the decline in Carter's support was fully nineteen percentage points, from 75 percent in 1976 to 56 percent in 1980" (Burnham, p. 108).

Although popular dissatisfaction with the income-maintenance programs played no large role in determining the outcome of the election, or in giving Reagan a mandate to slash them, the dissatisfaction is real. One source is the perception that social welfare programs encourage malingering, that they foster the poverty and dependency they are presumably designed to ameliorate. This is a very old view, expounded with particular vigor by nineteenth-century philanthropists during the period of rapid expansion by industrial capitalism, and for quite self-serving reasons, as we shall later note. Insofar as this is a popular view, it is not directed against programs that support the aged, although those are by far the most costly of the social welfare programs; nor is much animus directed against programs that support the disabled, or those that support the temporarily unemployed. Hostility is mainly directed against something people call "welfare," and what that means is Aid to Families with Dependent Children (AFDC). It must be said of this program that it does not account for very much of social welfare expenditures or for very many adult beneficiaries. Before the Reagan cuts, about $14 billion (including state and local shares) was spent to provide for slightly more than 11 million AFDC recipients, of whom more than 7 million were children.

Presumably the malingerers are among the 3.8 million adults

who are the mothers of these children. But those caring for the 36 percent of AFDC children under the age of 6 cannot be treated as malingerers, because most Americans would not endorse sending the mothers of small children out to work. Other mothers work while on the rolls, although at wages too low to bring them above AFDC eligibility levels, so they are not malingerers either. Still more have worked recently and will work again. Studies of the work patterns of AFDC family heads show that a good many women remain on welfare for only a short time to cope with temporary unemployment, illness, or other family crises, and their numbers would no doubt fall were unemployment levels to drop (27 percent have been on the rolls less than a year, and 55 percent less than three years). What remains, then, is the minority of AFDC mothers whose life situation has demoralized them, whose experience of unemployment and social disorganization has made them "dependent," and whose children may, if these conditions persist, grow up to be "dependent" as well. Welfare is not a good solution for these people. It may keep them from starving, but it does not enable them to reconstruct their self-respect. Eliminating welfare payments in the absence of other economic and social opportunities is, however, a worse solution.

Another basis for popular dissatisfaction with social welfare programs is that they constitute a bonanza to the bureaucratic special interest groups that provide particular services. This sort of criticism is made indiscriminately, sweeping in programs like Social Security and AFDC, where the "special interests" consist of rather lowly civil servants and their computers, and where administrative costs constitute only a small fraction of total program costs. But it does contain more than a grain of truth with respect to other programs, mainly those in health care and housing. These programs have improved the health of the poor, and the housing of some of the poor. However, they have been organized so as to facilitate their exploitation by the private entrepreneurs who provide the services. Medicare and Medicaid, the principal health programs, are essentially schemes to reimburse private providers for services delivered to the old and the poor. As a consequence, very large (and sometimes fraudulent) profits have been made by doctors, clinics, and nursing homes, and by secondary providers such as pharmaceutical and hospital equipment companies. Most housing programs, except for public housing, are similarly organized. Low-cost loans or rent subsidies are provided by government to encourage entrepreneurs to build and rent to low-income families. The essential principle is to make it profitable for private enterprise to provide services to low-income people. And profitable it is, as repeated scandals exposing builders who bilk both the government and the poor have revealed.

Profiteering in the social welfare state is not accidental. Housing and health care programs were designed in the face of pressures from special interests that stood to lose or gain. This pattern is a familiar one in American politics. The American Medical Association long resisted any form of government health insurance, for example; but when that resistance was overcome, the AMA used its still formidable lobbying power to ensure that the Medicare program for the aged would permit private vendors to charge customary fees. (Medicaid reimbursements for health care to low-income families are set according to a fixed scale, but vendors often deal with that obstacle to profit by multiplying the diagnostic and treatment procedures their low-income patients must endure.) In other words, the serious profiteering in government social welfare does not result from the growth of the public bureaucracy; it results from the vigor with which private economic interests exploit bureaucratic programs. (It is noteworthy that a number of European health and housing programs give less latitude to market interests, with moderating effects on program costs. But these programs were inaugurated or restructured at a time when the economies of these countries had been weakened by war, with the consequence that the health and housing industries of that time lacked the political influence to shape programs in their own interests.)

There are, in other words, problems in the welfare state programs. But no serious investigation of "fraud and abuse" would begin with the unemployment, food, and welfare programs. It might begin with defense contracts or the tax system, where fraud and profiteering are normal rather than merely rampant, and where the gains made are huge. And one might go on to the private vendors associated with the Medicare, Medicaid, and housing programs. For the Reagan administration, however, fraud and abuse are not the real issues, and the budget cuts are not directed against these problems. They are directed against the recipients of welfare state benefits.

The main political meaning of popular dissatisfaction with several of the income-maintenance programs is not that the Reagan administration had a mandate to cut them, but that it could begin to do so without risking much immediate opposition. Another comment by Burnham is pertinent here: "Opinion data consistently make the point that Americans are in the main eager to get the particularized benefits coming to them personally which the state offers. But they also make it clear that [the state that gives those benefits] is not well loved" (p. 121). And that state is loved least which gives benefits to the poor and unemployed. Still, the swing voters who put Reagan in office were urgently concerned that unemployment rates be reduced, not unemployment benefits. And even if many of those same swing voters thought that Carter should have cracked down on the alleged "abuses" in the welfare and food stamp programs, that is not why they deserted him. In other words, the main significance of popular ambivalence toward some of the income-maintenance programs is that it makes them vulnerable to attack. The Reagan administration also wanted to make substantial cuts in the Social Security system, but it pulled back because influential organizations of the aged protested. And so the overall attack was limited, for a time, to cutting those programs that enjoy less popular support and whose constituencies are ineffectively organized.

IF POPULAR SENTIMENT does not explain the Reagan assault on the welfare state, what then does? The programs that provide a national minimum-income floor are being cut back as one part of a larger strategy to increase business profits. The other parts of the strategy are easily described. The federal tax structure has been reorganized to promote a massive upward redistribution of income. New investment and depreciation write-offs favor large corporations over small businesses; 80 percent of the benefits go to the 1,700 largest corporations (which have generated only 4 percent of all new employment over the past twenty years). And personal income and estate taxes were slashed by formulas that give 85 percent of the benefits to those with annual incomes exceeding $50,000. An estimated $750 billion in federal revenue over the next five years has been forfeited, and cuts in the income-maintenance programs will help offset that lost revenue.

The Reagan administration also set out to save business and industry billions of dollars by undoing the apparatus through which government regulates business. The budgets and powers of agencies responsible for controlling the polluting effects of industry, enforcing health and safety standards in the workplace, overseeing guidelines for the hiring of women and minorities, prosecuting antitrust suits, and limiting the exploitation of mineral resources on federal lands, to mention a few, were all reduced or abolished. Directives were promulgated that explicitly relaxed enforcement standards and lowered the penalties for violations. The agencies were internally reorganized to remove stubborn bureaucrats from the scene of enforcement, and a new crop of officials was recruited, usually from the regulated industries.

And then there are the Reagan administration's foreign and military policies. The human-rights stance of the Carter administration has been abandoned, faltering and uncertain though it may have been, in favor of a belligerent posture of open support for right-wing dictatorships around the globe, on the ground that these "authoritarian" regimes are our allies in a world everywhere menaced by the expansionism of a "totalitarian" Soviet Union (thus justifying American expansionism). And the military budget is being raised to extraordinary levels, with expenditures expected to reach $346 billion by the last year of Reagan's term. From the perspective of profits, the consequences of the shift in foreign and military policies are mixed. Large increases in military expenditures work against the goal of lowering taxes and the professed aim of paring down "big government." Moreover, precipitous increases in military expenditures will probably have disruptive and inflationary effects as the military sector absorbs great quantities of materials and skilled labor, thus creating shortages and bottlenecks elsewhere in the economy, as Thurow and others have pointed out. But these problems aside, high levels of military expenditure also redistribute wealth and income upward because military industries are so capital-intensive. Moreover, an aggressive foreign policy is consistent with the goal of enlarging profits, for it would expand the reach of American business abroad if it succeeded.

Ordinarily, policies are complex, their effects mixed, and the

claims made for them often obscure their intended consequences. The current policies are bold and focused, however,
and their purpose is transparent. The combination of tax cuts
and regulatory relaxation is intended to increase the profits of
American business. If anyone were inclined to look for a deeper
motive, the Reagan administration's own frank paeans to profit
suggest no other will be found.

But the call for increased profits is not the whole of the
Reagan administration's justification. Nor could it be, since a
call for greater profits would not by itself win much citizen
support. Rather, the claim is that greater profits will lead to
greater prosperity by promoting the investment, entrepreneurial effort, and innovation that combine to produce
more jobs and rising real income for all. Or, as Reagan said,
quoting Theodore Roosevelt in an address to an audience of
the United Brotherhood of Carpenters and Joiners, "We must
decide that it is a great deal better that some people should
prosper too much than that no one should prosper enough."

This approach did not spring to life all at once in 1981.
Rather the Reagan administration has become the voice of a
decade-long campaign waged by the large corporations. Their
demands were expressed in such business organs as the *Wall
Street Journal, Fortune* magazine, and *Business Week,* and in
corporate advertisement-editorials. (Corporations now spend
approximately one-third of their tax-deductible advertising dollars to influence people as "citizens" rather than just as con-
sumers.) The message of the campaign was clear: the competitive position of American business in the world economy has
been undermined by what Mobil Oil, in one of its regular
advertisement-editorials, called "negative growth—growth in
taxes, government spending and burdensome regulation" resulting from "the era when government grew so fat and flabby
that its weight pulled the private sector right into the ground."

It is worthwhile to separate the rhetoric from the substance in such statements. The rhetoric consists of an attack on "big government," and this is an idea that resonates in American culture. But the Reagan program will not reduce the overall size of government, for the expansion of the military budget will more than offset budget cuts so that the scale of government will increase. And the expansion of the defense sector inevitably entails greater intrusion by government into the inner workings of the economy, since defense contractors become closely and intricately involved with the government agencies they supply. Even tax cuts are misleading. The capacity of the tax-state to shape economic and social life is not a consequence of the level of taxation alone. It is just as much a consequence of the way in which the complex forms and incidence of taxation influence the myriad private decisions that shape economic and social life. Grandiose plans for remilitarization and the fantastic complexities of the restructured tax system in fact represent new influences by the state on the larger society.

When the rhetoric about big government is put aside, Mobil's argument becomes clear, as does the argument of the Reagan administration. High taxes on large businesses and the wealthy reduce profitability and thus discourage investment. Government regulations shrink profits further by increasing the costs of doing business and inhibiting entrepreneurial innovation. Finally, continuing deficits cause government to borrow hugely in the capital markets, presumably driving up the cost of money, thus crowding out corporate borrowers and adding further to inflation as government increases the supply of money in order to finance its borrowing.

There is not much doubt that the Reagan policies will increase profits. What is doubtful is the promise that increased profits will lead to widespread economic improvement. There are real problems in the American economy; inflation and unemployment, which erode living standards, are symptoms of them. But there is no evidence that these problems result from a shortage of capital. Between 1960 and 1978 available corporate capital increased by 662 percent, according to Miller and Devey, and the annual rate of corporate savings did not decline either. In 1978 *Business Week* magazine reported that "the nation's biggest corporations are sitting atop a record $80 billion pile of cash that could finance a grand boom in capital spending." However, there was no boom in capital spending, for corporations have been channeling their profits into short-term financial markets and real estate ventures; into commodity futures that increased fiftyfold in value between 1960 and 1978 (Miller and Devey); into the mergers through which companies buy up other companies and raise speculative values without increasing productive capacities, a form of investment that, according to the *Wall Street Journal*, accounted for a record $61 billion and 1,807 transactions in the first nine months of 1981 alone; and into international investment, which increased twentyfold between 1950 and 1978, reaching $377 billion in 1978 (Ginsberg and Vojta). As a result, the United States lags behind Europe and Japan in its rate of investment in the domestic machinery, structures, and technology that increase productivity and employment.

This trend cannot be attributed to shortages of capital resulting from excessive taxes or from large government deficits. Not only is there no capital shortage, but effective rates of taxation on American business have been falling sharply for several decades. Nor is there evidence that the size of government deficits bears any regular relationship to productive investment. To be sure, lower taxes and less regulation will increase profits, and lower deficits will release capital. These policies may well spur investment, and they are likely to spur speculation as well. What they are not so likely to do is channel capital into investment in new domestic plant capacity. It is thus improbable that they will reverse the trends in capital flow associated with slower rates of growth in the productivity of the American economy and with the lower real incomes and higher unemployment that sluggish growth entails.

The underlying reasons for the reluctance of American corporations to make long-term investments in new productive capacity are rooted in deep changes in the international economy, and in America's role in the international economy. Those changes include the emergence of strong competitor economies in Western Europe and Japan, the pervasive shock of rising energy costs, the narrowing of investment and marketing opportunities in the Third World, and the increasingly precarious debt structure of international financial institutions strained by these developments. What these troubles signal overall is the shrinking or exhaustion of the extraordinary expansionist possibilities of the period following World War II when American capital, its competitors weakened by war, dominated the world. That brief era is over. This does not mean that American capitalism is now faltering on the edge of the ultimate crisis. It only means that the postwar boom has ended because the conditions that made it possible no longer exist. Comparable rates of growth are not likely to resume unless comparable opportunities for expansion emerge—such as greatly increased economic penetration of the socialist world. In the meantime, American corporations have been moving away from investment in the productive capacity that would generate employment and raise living standards by adopting a strategy favoring speculation and overseas investment.

The Reagan administration has not identified these problems, nor does its program solve them. Instead, the Reagan program identifies and solves the alleged problems of capital shortage and declining investment, neither of which appears to exist. And the way these alleged problems are to be solved is by reducing the share of the national product that goes to the working class—by cutting taxes on business and wealth, by dismantling government regulation of business, and by slashing the income-maintenance programs. The argument that taxes and government programs are to blame for the deep-rooted problems in the economy is a way of attempting to make this redistribution of wealth palatable to the American people. David Stockman, director of the Office of Management and Budget, conceded as much when he incautiously confided to a journalist that Reagan's tax bill was a "Trojan horse" full of tax benefits for the rich, and that supply-side economics is nothing but traditional Republican "trickle-down" economic theory in disguise (Greider). The slashing of the social programs is a crucial part of this strategy. If the tax cuts redistribute funds to business and the wealthy, reductions in the income-maintenance programs ensure that these funds will be taken from the incomes of the poor and the working class.

DIRECTLY REDISTRIBUTING INCOME upward is not the whole reason for slashing the income-maintenance programs. There is a more important but less obvious way in which profits will be enhanced by these cuts. *The income-maintenance programs are coming under assault because they limit profits by enlarging the bargaining power of workers with employers.* To unravel the relationship between the income programs and the power of working people in labor market relations, we need first to say a word about the way these programs are tilted toward the poor, and about their magnitude.

The welfare state developed much later in the United States

than in Western Europe, but it then expanded rapidly. The foundations were laid in 1935 with the enactment of Social Security pensions, unemployment insurance, and welfare payments for the blind, dependent children, and those of the aged poor not eligible for Social Security. Shortly afterwards, the federal program for public housing was enacted. In 1951, the permanently and totally disabled were also granted aid. These programs made up the initial income-maintenance framework of the American welfare state.

Although the foundation was laid in the 1930s, the great expansion and elaboration of income-maintenance programs did not occur until the 1960s and 1970s. From 1960 to the early 1970s, the number of people on the Aid to Families with Dependent Children rolls quadrupled. The food stamp program and other nutritional programs were enacted in these years; so was subsidized health care for the elderly (Medicare) and for welfare recipients and the working poor (Medicaid); housing subsidies, for public housing and for rent assistance, were also greatly enlarged. In 1973, the public welfare categorical assistance programs for the aged and disabled (but not for dependent children and their mothers) were absorbed into a new federal program called Supplemental Security Income (SSI), and a sharp rise in the disability rolls followed. Other disability programs also grew. Major new programs were also enacted in the 1970s. The Comprehensive Employment and Training Act (CETA) provided training and thousands of public service jobs for the unemployed. The Trade Adjustment Assistance Act made payments available to workers displaced from their jobs by foreign competition. And the Emergency Fuel Assistance Act provided funds for low-income families who could not pay rising fuel bills.

Federal expenditures in support of individual and family income were projected to reach $373 billion in fiscal 1982, plus

$25 billion in matching funds contributed by states and locali-
ties for Medicaid and AFDC (see table on pages 16–19). These
projected federal expenditures represented about 11.3 percent
of the $3.3 trillion 1982 estimated Gross National Product
(GNP).

Although American income-maintenance expenditures as a
percentage of GNP now approach levels prevailing in European social welfare states, the distribution of these benefits is
very different. American programs are tilted more toward the
bottom of the income scale. To be eligible for a number of
our programs—such as unemployment insurance, CETA,
food stamps, AFDC, SSI, and Medicaid—one must be
unemployed or otherwise lack income; that is, many American programs are "means-tested" or "unemployment-tested."
At the same time, the United States has had higher levels of
both unemployment and low-wage jobs, with the result that a
larger flow of funds is triggered through these means-tested
programs. Moreover, even Social Security pensions, though
not means-tested, are sharply redistributional, for half of the
money transferred goes to people who would otherwise fall
below the federal poverty line. Taken in the aggregate, all
cash and "in-kind" benefits (food, health care, and housing
subsidies) account for an average annual equivalent of $2,500
for each person who would otherwise fall below the poverty
line. Looked at another way, almost half of the aggregate income of the bottom fifth of the population is derived from
social welfare benefits. The poorest people in the country are
now as much dependent on the government for their subsistence as they are on the labor market.

It is mainly the downward tilt of the social programs that
attracted the Reagan budget axe. Non-means-tested programs
such as Social Security and Medicare and a variety of veterans'
benefits have been dealt with delicately and cautiously. The

Major Cuts in Income-Maintenance Programs
(as of September 26, 1981)

Program Description; Number of Participants Before Budget Cuts (latest available figures)	Fiscal 1982 Baseline* (in billions)	Fiscal 1982 Cuts (in billions)	How Principal Savings Achieved
Old Age, Survivors, and Disability Insurance (largest of all social programs). 20,500,000 *aged* 3,700,000 *dependents of aged* 7,000,000 *survivors under 65* 5,000,000 *disabled and dependents*	160.0	none	Minimum payment of $122 per month eliminated, but then restored. Disability rolls being audited, with potentially large future reductions. Early retirement benefits may be slashed, and age of retirement may be postponed to age 68.
Federal retirement, survivors, and disability. 1,000,000 recipients in all.	20.0	none	
Railroad retirement, survivors, and disability. 1,000,000 recipients in all.	5.8	none	
Military retirement, survivors, and disability. Beneficiary figures not available.	16.0	none	
Veterans retirement, survivors, and disability. 4,500,000 recipients in all.	13.7	none	
Supplemental Security Income (cash grants to low-income aged, blind, and disabled). 4,200,000 aged and disabled recipients.	8.0	−$ .05	Accounting methods tightened; national investigation of disability cases could lead to 20% reduction over next several years.

Black Lung (payments to miners disabled by pneumoconiosis).	1.9	none	
Medicare (federal program to pay for medical care for the aged).	46.6	none	
Medicaid (state-federal program to pay for medical care for the poor; about 40% goes to care for indigent aged). 18,000,000 beneficiaries.	18.5 (states add approximately equal amount)	−$ 1.1	Federal payments to states reduced. Most states will probably reduce their share as well.
Food Stamps (coupons good for food purchase, issued to low-income households). 22,600,000 beneficiaries	12.3	−$ 1.7	Income eligibility limited; inflation adjustments delayed; benefits to working poor reduced.
School Feeding Program (subsidies for meals served at school; additional subsidies for meals served to children from low-income families). 26,000,000 beneficiaries	$ 4.5	−$ 1.4	Federal subsidies cut; income eligibility limited; special milk program eliminated; summer feeding program restricted.
Supplemental Feeding for Women (food packages of eggs, dairy products, and fruits provided to low-income mothers and children deemed to be at "nutritional risk"). 2,200,000 beneficiaries.	$ 1.0	+$ .02	Spending not cut, but limited to $1.017 billion.
Aid to Families With Dependent Children (grants to state programs of cash support for low-income families with children). 11,100,000 recipients.	$ 6.6 (states add approximately equal amount)	−$ 1.2	Benefits to working recipients greatly reduced; states allowed to establish "workfare" programs.

Major Cuts in Income-Maintenance Programs (Cont.)
(as of September 26, 1981)

Program Description; Number of Participants Before Budget Cuts (latest available figures)	Fiscal 1982 Baseline* (in billions)	Fiscal 1982 Cuts (in billions)	How Principal Savings Achieved
Energy Assistance (grants to states for distribution to welfare recipients and other low-income families for help with energy bills). 11,700,000 households assisted.	$ 2.2	−$ .4	Spending limited to $1.875 billion. Program converted to block grant.
Housing Assistance (rent subsidies for low-income families; assistance to public housing). 2,400,000 households.	$28.6	−$11.6	Number of new subsidized units cut; higher rental contribution from tenants required.
Unemployment Insurance (federal-state insurance program providing 26 weeks of benefits to unemployed; extended benefits for additional 13 weeks available under certain conditions). Number of beneficiaries varies with economic conditions; 4,100,000 average weekly beneficiaries in Fiscal 1981.	$21.0	−$ .2	Nationwide extended benefits eliminated; restrictions placed on conditions under which states can provide extended benefits; after 13 weeks, unemployed must take any job offered.
CETA Public Service Jobs (grants to states and localities to provide jobs to low-income unemployed). 822,000 beneficiaries over the course of a year.	$ 3.8	−$ 3.8	Program eliminated.

| CETA Job Training and Youth Programs (grants to states and localities to provide job training to low-income youths and unemployed). 2,800,000 beneficiaries. | $ 2.6 | $ .6 | Spending limits enacted. |

TOTALS

1982 projected expenditures before cuts: $373.1 billion.

1982 projected expenditures before cuts as a percentage of the 1982 estimated Gross National Product of $3.3 trillion: 11.3 percent.

1982 cuts as of September 26, 1981: $22.05 billion.

1982 cuts as a percent of the programs that were cut: 20 percent.

* This baseline is, generally, the Congressional Budget Office's projection of the amount needed to maintain existing program levels in fiscal 1982, based on 1981 spending adjusted for inflation.

SOURCES: *Budget of the United States Government, Fiscal Year 1982* (the Carter budget); and *The Congressional Quarterly*, September 26, 1981.

brunt of the cuts falls on public service employment, unemployment insurance, Medicaid, public welfare, low-income housing subsidies, and the disability and food stamp programs.

THE CONNECTION BETWEEN the income-maintenance programs, the labor market, and profits is indirect, but not complicated. To see the connection, it is necessary to consider the relationship between unemployment and worker bargaining power. Large numbers of unemployed people exert a downward pressure on wages because people searching for work are forced to underbid the wages of those currently working. A mass of unemployed also inhibits workers from making other workplace demands; workers are less militant when there is a long line of job applicants outside the factory gates. Because the unemployed exert a downward pressure on wages and other labor costs, the existence of a large pool of unemployed tends to maintain and enlarge profits. (This effect is moderated by union contracts at one end of the wage scale and by minimum-wage laws at the other end, but it is not eliminated.) By contrast, when the unemployed are absorbed and labor markets tighten, wage and workplace demands push against profits, as some analysts say happened in the late 1960s at the climax of the long post–World War II boom (Duboff).

The relationship between unemployment and wage levels was described by Marx when he claimed the unemployed constitute an "industrial reserve army of labor" used by capitalists to weaken and divide the proletariat. But most American analysts scoffed at the notion that large-scale unemployment represented an advantage for capital, much less that this advantage was sometimes deliberately contrived. Instead, the fact that the United States has had consistently higher rates of unemployment than other Western industrial countries, except during wartime, was attributed by the more conservative analysts to "frictional" unemployment—that is, to the exceptional mobility of the American work force as people moved from job to job to take advantage of opportunities to improve their circumstances. Unemployment, in short, was taken to be a symptom of prosperity. High unemployment rates in the United States were also attributed to the composition of the labor force.

> The unemployed are an ever changing mass, on a kind of shuttle, moving and waiting, never fitting comfortably in any job, yet usually able to find another. This turbulence tracks back to shifts in the composition of the civilian labor force. . . . The number of adult white men, who have a low rate of unemployment, has been dwindling in relation to the total force. But teenagers, blacks, and women, who have high rates, have been joining in record numbers; surpris-

ingly, they now make up half its total. [Guzzardi, quoted in Schlozman and Verba, p. 31]

To make the point more clearly, the argument posits that prosperity enables many workers to circulate more freely from job to job as a means of improving their wages and working conditions. Prosperity also brings to the labor market large numbers of people who presumably do not seriously need or want work (teenagers, women, blacks), and their consequent job instability also contributes to an artificial appearance of high unemployment. Unemployment, in short, is caused by the unemployed themselves, an argument developed in purest form by Milton Friedman, who put forward the thesis that unemployment always settles at its "natural" rate over the long term.

Liberal analysts following Keynes developed a very different interpretation of unemployment, however. They fastened on overall levels of economic activity as the cause of joblessness. Unemployment was seen as the consequence of sluggish business and consumer demand. Tighter labor markets in turn were the result of swelling business and consumer demand. The significance of this perspective, which acquired much legitimacy in the post–World War II period, was that it defined unemployment levels as susceptible to regulation by government, for unemployment could be lowered by policies to stimulate aggregate demand.

But although high levels of aggregate demand are associated with lower unemployment rates, they are also associated with rising wage and price levels. And the very same formulation that led economists to think that unemployment levels could be controlled by government intervention to stimulate the economy also led them to think inflation could be controlled by government intervention to reduce aggregate demand. In other words, unemployment and inflation came to be seen as tradeoffs, for the one could only be controlled at the expense of the other. This formulation is embodied in the widely cited correlation between levels of unemployment and wage levels, published by Phillips in 1958, and known as the "Phillips Curve." When unemployment falls, wages rise; when unemployment rises, wages fall. The Phillips curve was thus consistent with Marx's thesis regarding the industrial reserve army of labor, for it suggested that high levels of unemployment weaken the bargaining power of workers. However, economists did not define the trade-off between unemployment and wages as a reflection of conflicts over the distribution of wealth; they tended instead to see it as describing a relationship existing in economic nature.

Economists were even sometimes saddened by this "natural" economic relationship. "No one is happy with the prospect of unemployment," we were told by Fiedler (a former assistant secretary of the Treasury for economic policy in the Ford administration), "but in order to regain control over inflation, there is no other way" (1975, p. 175). Moreover, the magnitude of unemployment must be considerable if economic laws are to do their work. Thus Fabricant (senior staff member, Bureau of Economic Research): "I do not mean to belittle the burden of unemployment, either on those who suffer it or on the consciences of the rest of us. . . ." Nevertheless, "only when the rate of unemployment threatens to rise to intolerable levels, will it be time to consider [lowering it]. This is not yet the prospect, in my view" (1975, p. 165).

This conception of an unemployment-inflation trade-off was incorporated as an instrument of American public policy in the years after the Great Depression. Government planners tried to moderate the extremes of the business cycle with fiscal and monetary policies that regulated aggregate demand. Instead of business cycles that careened from trough to peak to trough again, relatively moderate recessions occurred every few years which increased unemployment without pushing it to staggering levels. In turn, higher unemployment rates produced lower wage and price levels. Government interventions to promote intervals of something less than depression levels of unemployment thus became major instruments of economic stabilization, and the publication of the Phillips curve gave this strategy the legitimization of science.

But these efforts at macroeconomic stabilization were not as neutral as they seemed. In the trade-off between unemployment and price inflation, American policy makers consistently elected to keep unemployment higher and price levels lower than other Western countries. This tilt in the trade-off benefited capital and weakened wage earners. To be sure, when the relationships underlying the trade-off are scrutinized, unemployment and price inflation can be understood as alternative strategies by which capital tries to maintain and enlarge profit shares, for price inflation is a way of attempting to erode wage increases won in tight labor markets. From the perspective of capital, however, inflation is less successful than unemployment as a strategy to maximize profits. Workers in the more unionized and less competitive sectors of the economy can keep pace with price increases, with the consequence that large numbers of working people gain relatively greater shares as the business cycle sweeps upward and the number of unemployed contracts. Cost-of-living escalator clauses in union contracts (some of which also cover pensions) institutionalize this power, reducing the effectiveness of price inflation in maintaining or enlarging profit shares. The indexing of Social Security benefits to inflation also results in higher employer costs, since payroll tax rises must be legislated to keep pace with benefits. Under these circumstances, inflation is relatively less effective in eroding the wage and benefit gains won in tight labor markets.

Douglas Hibbs presents evidence that is persuasive in this regard. He reviews a series of studies that examine the distribution of income in Western countries whose macroeconomic policies emphasize holding down unemployment and letting inflation rise, compared with countries whose policies emphasize holding down inflation and letting unemployment rise. The evidence, he concludes, strongly indicates that policies of lower unemployment and higher inflation lead to substantial improvement in the economic well-being of the poor and, "more generally, exert powerful equalizing effects on the distribution of personal income" (p. 1468). Moreover, as one would expect, these redistributional effects follow the business cycle: shares of the national income going to business increase steadily after a trough in business activity and reach their peak about midway in the upward sweep of the cycle; thereafter the business share drops off markedly (p. 1469). These findings suggest that inflation does not entirely offset the gains labor is able to make when unemployment levels are low.

Furthermore, price inflation is an insecure and cumbersome solution to the profit squeeze produced by tight labor markets and rising wage levels in other ways. It greatly complicates corporate dealings with suppliers and customers, and interferes with long-term corporate investment and planning, because of the uncertainties it generates. Domestic inflation is also disadvantageous in marketing goods in a world economy. For all of these reasons, the better way to maintain profits is to drive labor costs down, and for that, unemployment is the classic means. And it was just this strategy that predominated in American postwar economic policy.

For two decades following World War II, all seemed well. The relationship embodied in the Phillips curve varied to order, as Haveman shows for the period from 1952 to 1968, when cyclical increases in unemployment rates were matched by the expected fall-off in the rate of wage and price increases (p. 49). Then, toward the end of the 1960s, the relationship began to erode as prices spiraled upward despite high levels of unemployment. By the early 1970s, the relationship between unemployment and wage and price levels had disappeared. Barry Bosworth, head of Carter's Council on Wage and Price Stability in 1977–1979, comments on this development when he says that an unemployment rate of 6 percent failed to have an effect on inflation in the recession of 1969–1971:

> Economists, at first, viewed the problem as one of lags in the response of prices and wage rates; they recommended patience and a continuation of restrictive policies. By the beginning of 1971, however, *wage rate increases had actually accelerated slightly despite the high unemployment;* and, once excess inventories had been disposed of, the rate of price increases also picked up. [pp. 60–61; our emphasis]

Government economic stabilization policies failed, in short, because price and wage levels could no longer be moderated by raising unemployment.

The spiraling of prices in the later 1960s and the 1970s had a variety of sources. An early stimulus was the spurt in aggregate demand generated by high military spending (without offsetting tax increases) during the Vietnam War. Another inflationary stimulus was the surge in energy prices that pervaded an economy organized around low-cost fuel consumption. Increasing speculation, declining rates of investment in productive capacity, and monopoly pricing practices were yet more factors that contributed to the unprecedented inflation. Considering the magnitude of these forces, it is perhaps not surprising that price levels were immune to the deflationary effects of rising unemployment.

The surprise is that wage levels were also immune. Given the history of business cycles, one might have expected that even in the context of an inflationary environment produced by exceptional forces, high levels of unemployment would at least have restrained wage demands, thus reducing this component of prices. And government planners strove to produce just that effect. Throughout the 1970s, unemployment rose and remained at the highest levels since the 1930s. But despite the weakening of the labor market, wages did not fall. Something had happened to disrupt the traditional relationship between unemployment and wage levels, between the supply of labor and the power of labor. Or, in another idiom, the reserve army of labor was no longer performing its historic function.

HAVING MADE THESE various points, we come now to the relevance of the income-maintenance programs to the bargaining power of workers in the labor market. The timing of the disruption of the unemployment/wage-level trade-off coincided with the great expansion of social welfare benefits in the late 1960s and the 1970s, and that is suggestive. What it suggests is that income-maintenance benefits support wage levels despite high unemployment. The reason is simple. If the desperation of the unemployed is moderated by the availability of various benefits, they will be less eager to take any job on any terms. In other words, an industrial reserve army of labor with unemployment benefits and food stamps is a less effective instrument with which to deflate wage and workplace demands.

Many economists have recognized this. They now attribute the breakdown in the relationship between unemployment levels and wage levels to the great expansion of the income-maintenance programs. As Haveman recently put it, the unemployed can now "prolong job search . . . , refuse to accept work except at higher offered wages or cease active labor market participation" (p. 46). Bosworth concurs:

> [Traditional policies to restrain inflation] are guided by the need to create a pool of unemployed sufficient for the threat of lost sales or jobs to exert an adequate restraint on wages and prices. Economists have been engaged in long technical debate over the required size of the pool if price stability is to be maintained. But if the unemployed refuse to accept such a role, if they press for compensation and will be satisfied only when there is no economic penalty for not working, they will pose no threat to the employed. [pp. 69–70]

And Fiedler reaches the same conclusion:

> A change has taken place in the unemployment-inflation trade-off since the mid-1950s. [One reason] is the unemployed of today are subject to less economic pain than used to be the case, because of the development of more generous income-maintenance programs. . . . Consequently, most people who lose their jobs today are under less pressure to accept the first offer they get regardless of the pay and working conditions. [1979, p. 117]*

This conclusion is exclusively about wage levels, which are readily measured. But the effect of the income-maintenance programs in reducing economic insecurity and increasing the power of workers is not restricted to wage levels. Because

*Many analysts have attempted to estimate the magnitude of the overall reduction in work effort by the recipients of all kinds of income-maintenance payments. In an exhaustive review of more than 100 of these studies, the tentative conclusion is reached that the reduction in hours worked by transfer recipients may be equal to as much as 4.8 percent of the total hours worked by *all* workers, and that is a very considerable effect (Danziger, Haveman, and Plotnik, p. 996).

insecurity makes workers vulnerable, it also saps their strength
to make other demands in the workplace. When people fear
for their subsistence, they accept onerous and dangerous working conditions. They work harder, and they work longer. They
more readily accept discipline, follow orders, and submit to
humiliation. An insecure labor force is thus a more productive
labor force and a cheaper one, quite apart from wage levels.
(The new regulations denying food stamps to striking workers,
and to entire welfare families when a working member goes on
strike, seem intended to have exactly this disciplining effect.)
Conversely, a labor force that is made more secure by the
possibility of alternative means of subsistence is less docile, less
productive, and more costly.

These labor-market effects of the income-maintenance programs are surely of large significance. And if these effects are
causing mainstream and conservative analysts to worry, so
might analysts on the left have been expected to notice the
possibility that the welfare state had enlarged working-class
power. Until very recently, however, most of the left seemed
oblivious to the rapid and precipitous expansion of social welfare, tending to the opinion that social welfare programs in the
United States are insignificant compared to European programs. However, the benefits available are anything but insignificant; they are a force of indisputable importance in the
American political economy. Nor is it true, as many of the left
suppose, that the income-maintenance concessions won in the
1960s were pared down when protests subsided in the early
1970s (although that is now happening in the 1980s). To
be sure, the AFDC rolls stopped expanding, but the Medicaid rolls continued to rise, the food stamp rolls ballooned
after liberalizing amendments were added in 1971, Social
Security payments climbed more rapidly (by about 4 percent
a year in real terms), and a series of job-creation programs
was legislated. These facts cannot be brushed aside as insig-

nificant or merely symbolic. They demand serious appraisal.

Even the serious appraisals made by left analysts have not led to an understanding of the central role played by income-maintenance programs in strengthening the bargaining power of working people. The broad theme in neo-Marxist analyses is that social welfare programs are "functional" for capitalism (Miller, Devey, and Devey). Some analysts see social welfare programs as an instrument of economic stabilization in advanced capitalist societies: the programs serve to stimulate aggregate demand and to organize such essential requirements as transportation and housing, which can no longer, in a concentrated and complex economy, be left to the anarchy of the private market (Castells). Social welfare programs, in other words, are determined by the imperatives of the capitalist mode of production.

Other left critics argue that the welfare state arose from the need to pacify and depoliticize insurgent or potentially insurgent groups.* The yielding of social welfare programs is thus seen as part of the strategy by which the ruling class rules, a strategy through which working people are induced to cash in their political capacities and political intelligence for a pittance in material benefits. With the expansion of these programs, the body politic presumably grows more compliant, listless, and enfeebled. And as popular politics weakens, the state bureau-

*In *Regulating the Poor*, which was concerned only with poor relief or public welfare, we also argued that the expansion of public welfare was forced by the need to control an unruly poor during periods of mass unemployment. However, we saw such expansion as cyclical, as a temporary concession sometimes made to a turbulent mass of unemployed. We attributed an economic function to public welfare as well, but the economic function was not served by the expansion of welfare. It was served by a restrictive, punitive, and minimalist relief system, which forced most of the poor to offer themselves in the labor market on any terms, and which held up the pauper to public ridicule. As we noted in the Introduction to this essay, however, we now think the cyclical relief pattern may represent a characterization truer of the past than of the future.

cracies—imagined as monoliths of a far-seeing and cunning intelligence—rule America in collusion with their business allies (Wolin). This, in brief, is the left view of the corporate liberal state.

James O'Connor has brought these diverse critiques together in a coherent and influential functionalist argument (1973). O'Connor proposes that social welfare programs can be explained in terms of the basic imperatives that mold the activities of the state in a capitalist society. These imperatives, or "functions," consist of the need to ensure profitability or "accumulation" and the need to maintain sufficient social harmony so as to "legitimate" a class society and a class state. Social welfare programs presumably contribute to profitability by lowering the costs to employers of maintaining a healthy and skilled labor force. Without these programs, employers would either have to pay for health and education services directly, or raise wages to permit workers to purchase them. Social welfare programs also contribute to the legitimation function by quieting discontent, particularly the discontent generated by processes of economic concentration that create "surplus" labor, or unemployment.

However, O'Connor's model differs from other left views because it is not ultimately functionalist in the sense of characterizing a system in equilibrium. Rather, he points to the multiple crisis tendencies generated by the transference of conflicts between labor and capital to the state sector, and particularly by the fiscal crisis that results as state expenditures increase more rapidly than the revenues to finance them. In a similar vein, Gough claims that the scale of state expenditures for social welfare has become "a fetter on the process of capital accumulation. . . . If capitalism more and more engenders a welfare state, it is also proving difficult for capitalism to cope with the problem of financing the requisite expenditures" (p. 14).

These qualifications aside, the major thrust of left views has been that welfare state programs exist because their economic or their political effects are functional for capitalism. Recently, however, some left analysts have begun to see that the welfare state has not turned out to be functional for capitalism at all. Juliet Schor proposes that social welfare programs, "by providing extra-market means of subsistence . . . disrupt the functioning of the structures which currently reproduce the domination of labor by capital" (p. 4). Bowles and Gintis go further when they claim that the social programs have had the consequence of shifting labor and business income shares in the United States. And we ourselves wrote several years ago: "The expanding role of government in the distribution of income is evidence of a major transformation in the American political economy. It is a transformation that clearly enlarges the market leverage of American workers, particularly lower stratum workers, who are more likely to find themselves unemployed, and who are more susceptible to competition from the unemployed" (1979).

In short (and allowing for differences of terminology), there is an emerging recognition among analysts of all political persuasions that the income-maintenance programs have weakened capital's ability to depress wages by means of economic insecurity, especially by means of manipulating the relative numbers of people searching for work. In effect, these programs have altered the terms of struggle between business and labor. As a result, unemployment has lost some of its terrors, both for the unemployed and for those currently working. Despite unemployment rates in the 1970s ranging from 6 and 10 percent (not counting 1 million "discouraged" workers), there has been no significant downward pressure on wage levels. Economists now generally agree that it requires an increase in unemployment of at least a million individuals for a two-year period to reduce inflation by a single percentage point (Bosworth, p. 64). Because of the income-maintenance programs, in short, the reserve army is no longer quite so ready and willing to be called up in defense of profits.

Still, this discovery is not a discovery at all. Government programs that distribute income in one form or another have always altered the terms on which people would work, and that is not a discovery of supply-side economics, of Marxist economics, or of any other brand of economics. This effect has been apparent since the emergence of "free markets" in which most people were forced to sell their labor to a few in order to obtain adequate subsistence. When people had an alternative means of subsistence, they were not as likely to sell their labor except under terms that improved their situation, and they were less likely to accept the most backbreaking or degrading forms of work. This relationship has been understood whether the alternative subsistence was given in the form of bread and coal, as it once was, or in the form of cash, nutritional supplements, housing subsidies, and health care, as it now is. It has been understood whether the benefits were called "poor relief," as they once were, or "income-maintenance programs," as they now are. In short, it has always been recognized that the most effective way to "regulate the poor" in the labor market is to close off access to alternative means of subsistence.

THREE GENERAL EFFECTS will follow the reduction of subsistence resources: economic insecurity will be intensified among the unemployed; large numbers of persons now exempted from work will be thrown into the labor market, thus creating additional unemployment; and economic insecurity among the working poor will be greatly worsened.*

Reducing the number of weeks during which those out of work can collect unemployment assistance and trade-adjustment assistance benefits will strip workers already searching for work of protections, and the threat of expiring benefits will make them bid sooner for any job on any terms. That process will be accelerated by new regulations requiring that benefits be terminated after thirteen weeks for unemployed workers who refuse to accept available jobs, even jobs offering lower wages and requiring lower skills than their customary employment. It is hard to offer precise estimates of the scale of these effects, for the answer depends partly on the vigor with which the Reagan administration pushes implementation of the new rules. If, for example, the unemployment rolls were to remain at the weekly average of 4 million that prevailed in 1981, program changes forcing 10 percent off the rolls would result in an additional 400,000 unemployed workers without protections, and a 25 percent reduction would result in a million unprotected workers.

The termination of the CETA public service jobs program precipitately threw almost 400,000 new unemployed onto the labor market. Changes in the AFDC program will add more.

---

*Different methods of depriving people of benefits are being instituted. Some methods are visible and their effects calculable, but others are not. Some will produce immediate effects, others longer-term effects. If programs are simply abolished, the visible and immediate effects can readily be assessed. If eligibility rules are formally changed by statute or bureaucratic regulation, these effects too are sufficiently visible and immediate to make estimates possible. By contrast, much of the cost-cutting will occur by tightening up bureaucratic processes for determining eligibility: systematic post-audits of existing caseloads will be conducted, and new applications will be scrutinized differently. The way bureaucratic functionaries exercise discretion in determining initial or continuing eligibility is very much influenced by shifts in the political climate. The magnitude of the effects of such changes in the exercise of bureaucratic discretion can be known only by waiting for the periodic statistical reports from these agencies regarding the rates of applications approved as well as the rates of termination. But the direction is clear enough.

AFDC children between the ages of 18 and 21 were previously permitted to remain on the rolls if they attended school; under Reagan, states may at their option continue to distribute benefits to the 18-year-olds who are in school, but the 19- and 20-year-olds are now disqualified no matter whether they are in school. That will add about 100,000 to the youth unemployment rolls, and it will cause about 25,000 families in which the 19- or 20-year-old is the only child to lose AFDC benefits. And then there is "workfare": an as yet unknown number of AFDC heads-of-families will be forced into workfare programs, where they will do the work for which county and municipal governments would otherwise recruit workers who would demand regular pay and fringe benefits. Eligibility criteria are also being made more restrictive, with the result that initial acceptance rates will also fall and termination rates will rise, keeping hundreds of thousands of destitute family heads in the labor market searching for work.

Most disabled people were once workers; many will be again. There, are 6 million people between the ages of 21 and 64 (not including disabled veterans) who subsist on one or another system of federal disability payments. Whether someone is too disabled to work is almost always a matter of judgment, and the exercise of judgment is in turn influenced by larger policy goals. The goal now is to cut the rolls. Having reviewed samples of cases, the Social Security Administration claims to have found 38 percent "ineligible," and the conclusion is that a minimum of 20 percent—or more than 1 million persons—can be pruned from the rolls. To this end, a nationwide Continuing Disability Investigation has been launched, and large numbers of the disabled have already received termination notices. (One immediate result has been a sharp upsurge of appeals; so far these appeals have produced a reversal rate of over 50 percent, which high officials in the Social Security Administration are defining as "unacceptable." The contemplated solution is to eliminate "vocational" criteria, such as age and education, in the determination of disability. Thus, a 60-year-old male elementary school graduate with a cardiac problem who has always performed unskilled labor would be considered fit for work on the ground that he can do sedentary work. With vocational criteria thus eliminated, the disability rolls could perhaps be cut by as much as half.)

Finally, enormous long-term increases in unemployment could result from changes in Social Security. Social Security took old people out of a labor force that did not have much use for them. It also freed the young from having to compete with the old for the low wages for which the old could be hired. But if the partial benefits that permit people to retire at age 62 are reduced (more than half of those eligible now elect early retirement), or if people are made to wait until age 68 to obtain full benefits, millions of the indigent aged will remain at work or join the search for work. That will be a hardship for many of them, and it will also be a hardship for the young who have to compete with them. It will be a hardship for younger working people in another way: they will have to devote a larger share of their earnings to the support of their aged parents, not least for medical care.

Finally, the working poor will also feel the brunt of the budget cuts. Some 400,000 families with a working head are to be lopped from the AFDC rolls, owing to the abolition of various "earned income disregards" and new limitations on "work expense disregards." Consequently, they will lose supplemental aid to their low incomes (half of these families earn less than $400 per month), and will end up with less income than non-working AFDC families. Furthermore, they and a great many non-welfare working-poor families will lose Medicaid, food stamps, and a portion of their housing subsidies because of new eligibility restrictions. The working poor enjoy minimal economic security only because of these food, medical, and housing supplements. With such benefits gone, many families will be forced to send spouses and children into the labor force to recoup the loss. Taking all of these "reforms" together, in other words, economic insecurity will increase sharply, and the situation will become even worse if the Reagan administration succeeds in obtaining large additional budget cuts in subsequent years.

Changes in the social programs will affect wages and profits in different parts of the economy. Labor markets are differentiated; so are the income-maintenance programs. On the one hand, the scaling down of unemployment and trade assistance benefits, together with the elimination of food stamps and Medicaid benefits for many workers, will intensify economic insecurity in most sectors of the work force, including the highly industrialized and unionized sectors. Two British economists make clear how reducing the total benefits available to the unemployed affects wage levels. Writing in *Lloyd's Bank Review*, they recite the advantages that would ensue from a 15 percent cut in unemployment payments. For one, the British government would save £3 million annually. And although cutting payments would "hit the least well-off, the indirect effect would be to lower real wages" which, in turn, would "spread employment to the unemployed" at lower wages. (And if early retirement benefits are cut or if the age of retirement is deferred, many older workers in the industrialized and unionized sector will remain in the work force, thus heightening the scramble for jobs and exerting pressure for lower wages.)

On the other hand, much of the unemployment produced by the scaling down of the programs for the disabled and AFDC families will affect mainly the large and fast-growing service sector of the economy. This sector will also feel the main effects of cuts in the Social Security program. The rolls of all of these programs are disproportionately composed of unskilled women—younger women in the AFDC program, and older women in the other programs. Contrary to popular impressions (and some academic ones: see Ginzburg and Vojta, for example), the service sector is not populated mainly by educated and skilled workers. Rothschild reports that more than 70 percent of all new private jobs created between 1973 and 1980 were in services and retail trades alone; and within these, employment growth was concentrated in eating and drinking establishments, which include the mammoth fast-food chains, and in health and business services, which include "services to buildings," such as offices and hotels. This huge and expanding sector of the economy relies on a vast army of low-wage workers, the majority of them women who cook, serve, and clean. Cuts in the income-maintenance programs (including the loss of food stamps and Medicaid benefits) will have a large impact on working conditions in this sector, making service workers even more susceptible to onerous working conditions, as well as weakening their ability to maintain real wages in the face of inflation.

THROUGHOUT THIS ANALYSIS, we have attributed a rational calculus to the Reagan administration's assault on the income-maintenance programs. The problem of determining whether political leaders understand and intend the effects they create is always a delicate one. Although officials in the Reagan administration have not, of course, publicly stated that they intend to drive wages down by creating more unemployment and economic insecurity, it is nevertheless the case that the labor-market effects of the income-maintenance programs are understood by many analysts, including prominent economists associated with government either as employees or as recipients of government research funds in private "think tanks." We have mentioned a number of them in earlier pages. Martin Anderson, Reagan's chief domestic policy advisor and an acknowledged welfare expert and critic, should be added to the list. Reagan (as well as others in his administration) is said to swear by George Gilder's book *Wealth and Poverty*, which contains a full inventory of the usual criticisms of the income-maintenance programs, especially their deleterious effects on the work ethic. Analyzing the impact of the income-maintenance programs on the economy has become a growth industry among economists and social commentators, and the national administration could hardly fail to be influenced by the resulting climate of professional opinion.

Less rational calculations are also moving the Reagan administration. Reagan himself has shown enormous animus toward those he perceives to be enemies of the kind of social order he thinks he deserves to rule. As governor of California, he called black rioters "mad dogs," and insisted on cutting the already underfunded food budgets of mental institutions. He and his top appointees use a great deal of rhetoric about "fraud" and "malingering," and about benefits going to people for whom they were not intended, all of which leaves the clear implication that these "abuses" have created a government fiscal crisis. Reagan appears to believe that the "rabble" has captured the state and is plundering its resources, both to avoid work and to live better than those who do work. Productive people (like the self-made millionaires who surround Reagan) must be restored to honor, and to power. Thus does the indulgence of ideological animus nicely fit the calculation of class interest.

Indeed, when the several major policy initiatives of the Reagan administration are laid side by side, something of a coherent theory can be detected. But it is not a coherent theory of the workings of the economy. Economic thought has taken on the character of medieval theological disputation as economists of various faiths argue the true nature, causes, and probable effects of various Reagan policies and practices. Instead, the coherent theory is about human nature, and it serves the class interests of the Reagan administration and its business allies. It is the archaic idea that people in different social classes have different human natures and thus different basic motivations. The affluent are one sort of creature and working people another. It follows that these different sorts of creatures require different systems of incentives and disincentives if they are to be prodded to greater economic effort. The affluent exert themselves in response to rewards—to the incentive of increased profitability yielded by lower taxes. Working people respond only to punishment—to the economic insecurity that will result from reductions in the income support programs. It was just such a theory that nineteenth-century British political economists relied upon to justify the accumulation of riches by the few and the accumulation of misery by the many. The basic assumption of classical *laissez-faire* economic theory—that all people are rational and self-interested—was thus twisted to mean that the rationality and self-interest of the great majorities who were poor could be activated only by economic insecurity.

In the face of this theory, the growth of the welfare state was a considerable achievement. In simple and human terms, the welfare state has reduced some of the hardships and insecurities generated by a continually changing market economy that sloughs off the people it no longer needs like any other surplus commodity. People have not usually thought of themselves as surplus commodities; they have sometimes believed they had a right to subsistence. And when they did, they fought for that right. The programs of the welfare state are the fruits of these struggles. Moreover, these programs have turned out to be an achievement in another and more fundamental way that does more than protect the subsistence of those whose market position is weakest. The income-maintenance programs of the welfare state have expanded to the point where they intrude upon the dynamics of the labor market, augmenting the power of workers. And that is why they have become the target of a concerted attack by the privileged and powerful.

2

THE
ORIGINS
of the
CONFLICT

*T*HE MAIN PURPOSE of this book is to predict the outcome of the current assault on the social programs. Our prediction, however, is based on developments rooted in the past, even the distant past. So that our search in the past will not seem diversionary, we pause here to outline the general argument that will follow.

The contemporary corporate stake in slashing the income-maintenance programs is large. But that is not new. What is at issue in this struggle has been at issue since the rise of labor markets several centuries ago, as we explain in this chapter. Employers have always understood that subsistence resources interfere with wage labor. Indeed, labor markets did not become widespread in the first place until most of the subsistence resources of the pre-industrial community had been eliminated. To be sure, the old custom of charity persisted in the form of poor relief, but poor relief was the object of continuing contention as employers attempted to limit and shape relief-giving so as to enlarge their power in wage-labor relations. This history points up the centrality of the current struggle. What has flared up in our time is nothing less than the recurring conflict between property rights and subsistence rights, which originated with the emergence of capitalism itself.

In these past struggles, employers always ultimately won. And nowhere was their victory more total than in the United States, where the giving of relief to people while they lived in their own homes ("outdoor relief") was virtually eliminated by the close of the nineteenth century. The only public recourse that remained was the workhouse or the poorhouse, and this despite severe depressions and widespread hardship.

We often take domination for granted and think it is the resistance to domination that must be explained. The domination of government by the propertied also demands explanation, and especially in the United States, the first nation where political rights were widely extended. In other Western nations, demands by ordinary people for the franchise were long warded off. Here, however, white working-class men had the vote virtually from the beginnings of the republic. They were party to the spellbinding idea that the state belonged to the people, and to the vaulting promise of a better life inherent in that idea. But the idea and the promise were thwarted.

In chapter 3, we outline the ideological and institutional developments through which the promise was thwarted. Democratic rights did not enable ordinary people to act upon the most urgent economic problems in their lives because, even as political rights were won, the doctrine of *laissez faire* gained ascendance. This doctrine held that economic relationships were determined by natural "laws" with which neither the state nor the majorities that came to participate in the state should interfere. Political rights were thus separated from economic rights, and the economic experiences of ordinary people were made to have little bearing on their ideas about politics, or on their practice of politics, at least until the Great Depression. The world of the market was in effect shielded from the world of politics to which common people had gained some access.

This was a remarkable development. It was remarkable in part because *laissez faire* represented a radical departure from the experiences and ideas of the pre-industrial community in which economic and political roles had been fused (and where ideas about economics and politics had been fused). In the pre-industrial community, significant claims of the common people on political authority had to do with their economic condition. Political rights consisted mainly of economic rights, such as the right to use the land, or to work at a trade, or to receive charity in times of need. And it was precisely these traditional economic rights that were barred from the realm of politics in which democratic rights had been ceded.

The rise of an ideology that divided politics from economics was also remarkable because it triumphed at the historical moment when the idea of democracy was firing the popular imagination. To common people, democracy represented a solution to the economic grievances that accompanied the rise of mercantile and industrial capitalism. Of course, the people of Europe and America who fought for democratic rights wanted protection from coercion by the state. But they also wanted protection from coercion by the propertied. The idea of democracy embodied twin visions of a more just world. And while something of one vision was realized, nothing of the other was. Ordinary people participated in government, but that participation left them helpless in economic contests. They could not even prevent government from sending troops against them to crush their strikes, or their demands for poor relief. Thus was the promise of democracy defeated.

In the course of the twentieth century, the doctrine of separation weakened, and in chapter 4 we explain why. Grievances against property increasingly took the form of protests directed against the state. The broad movement by common people to exercise political rights in behalf of economic rights culminated in the great popular struggles of the 1930s and 1960s—in mass protests by the unemployed, industrial workers, the aged, blacks, and women. Politics and economics fused in the granting of federal emergency relief to the masses of unemployed, in collective-bargaining legislation, in wages-and-hours laws, in unemployment insurance, in pensions for the aged and disabled, in the enactment of public welfare subsidies for the unemployable, in occupational health and safety standards, in medical and housing programs, in civil rights legislation and affirmative action programs, and in a spate of general environmental protections.

These were developments of great significance. The doctrine of separation had more or less collapsed; when it did, political rights became the means by which ordinary people could and did act on the most pressing issues of their lives. Through the exercise of political rights, people succeeded in making the state the major arena of class conflict. Democracy finally offered people some defense against the historic alliance of state and capital—some protection against strikebreaking, against the hazards of the workplace, against discrimination by race and sex, and against the unemployment and destitution that had always made people desperate enough to take any job on any terms.

These twentieth-century developments were made possible

by profound and lasting changes in the American political economy, and that is why we are persuaded that the current mobilization against the welfare state will fail. The distinctive American political institutions of the nineteenth century shielded the various ways in which the state served capital from public view, and thus gave the ideology of *laissez faire* a certain credibility. But in the twentieth century, the penetration of the economy by the state on behalf of business has so expanded that the hypocrisy of *laissez faire* is more transparently evident. It is no longer possible to sustain a doctrine prescribing the separation of economy and polity, if only because it is so patently at odds with the reality. The Reagan administration may rail against interference in the economy by "big government," but what it actually means to condemn and eliminate is government interference on behalf of ordinary people, not government interference on behalf of business. The Reagan program is thus based on the premise that people are stupid, and that premise has proved wrong before.

Our prediction in chapter 5 that the enactments of the Reagan administration seem likely to provoke broad popular resistance is thus derived from an analysis of the changing interaction of ideology and institutional structures in American history. In order to present this analysis, however, we must turn first to the issue that is at the center of the current struggle (as it has been at the center of past struggles). That issue concerns the relationship of subsistence resources to employment and unemployment, and it is best illuminated by recalling the way labor markets were first brought into being and were then sustained.

FOR MOST PEOPLE through remembered time, work was taken for granted. Work was the struggle for subsistence and, excepting natural calamity or war, the resources through which human effort yielded subsistence were usually available. Most people were peasants of one kind or another, and they worked and earned their subsistence by tilling the land, and sometimes by handicrafts as well. The lives of peasants were usually mean, filled with unrelieved toil for only the barest livelihood, lived out in the shadow of devastation from natural disasters and sometimes from external aggression. Nor were peasants ordinarily independent in the sense of being free from domination by others. Whether serfs or servants or tenants or small proprietors, they were usually made to give up a portion of the products of their toil to their princes or lords or masters or landlords. Peasants lived shackled, in Hobsbawm's words, by the "double chains of lordship and labour" (1981, p. 2).

In this traditional order, Time conspired with God to teach fatalism, for both Time and God made the experiences of men and women seem inevitable. But there was more than Time, God, and fatalism. There were also ideas about how men and women should behave toward one another, and toward those of different stations in the context of a world dominated by Time and God. In communities where existence was precarious and where scarcity and violence always threatened, these ideas, and the standards of justice in human relations that they generated, cemented the peasant to the social order because they dealt with the essential and preoccupying question of subsistence. While some were rich and most were poor, the rich had a responsibility to ensure the subsistence of the poor that tempered their authority, and the poor had a right to subsistence that mitigated the burden of their duties to the rich. These mutual duties and rights acquired their force because they were perceived to organize and protect subsistence and to offer some shield against the calamity of dearth that always stalks those who live at the edge of subsistence.

But whatever else may be said of the travails that marked the lives of most people throughout history, the search for employment and the fear of unemployment, as we understand these experiences, were not among them. Work was an organic part of the unending order of things, linked to subsistence, and to the material resources from which it yielded sustenance.

Labor markets did not, as is sometimes thought, evolve naturally from this traditional order through the mutual adjustment of different people to changing relationships and changing circumstances. Labor for hire was usually a system that was imposed, often with brutal force. Because their lives were filled with drudgery and the threat of natural disaster, some peasants left traditional communities to improve their lives by selling their labor. But the usual notion that throughout history great tides of people left the land—whether of Lancashire or of New England or of Puerto Rico—because they were attracted by the opportunity or excitement of urban life is incorrect. Most people did not, and still do not, enter the market voluntarily. They did not and do not voluntarily give up their ties to place and kin, or the rhythms of a life they know, for the entirely alien and unknown, and, more to the point, they did not give up these things for the grueling work, the regimentation, and the low wages that characterized emerging labor markets.

Most people were forced into the labor market because their traditional means of work and subsistence were simply taken from them. Sometimes the time-honored right to work the land was wrested from them; sometimes new encroachments on the peasants' share of the product eroded their narrow margin of survival. Only when the traditional nexus of work and subsistence was broken did most people enter the labor market. And those who became the employers in the new labor markets—the landowners of a commercializing agriculture that required seasonal labor, or the masters of the putting-out system of early capitalism, or the factory owners of industrial capitalism—usually understood that the way to create a pool of labor for hire among a reluctant peasantry was to eliminate the traditional means of subsistence, whether by overriding customary rights to the common lands or the forests, by increasing rents or dues or taxes, or by "freeing" serfs only to eject them from the land they had tilled. By these strategies, many millions of people over the centuries were pushed into wage labor on penalty of starvation. They were forced into a relationship in which subsistence was made conditional, not on work itself, but on employment by those who owned the resources that labor turned into valued goods.

The encroachment by the propertied classes on subsistence resources was not always motivated by their need for wage labor. The displacement of people from the pre-industrial community was often merely the by-product of the simple appetite for wealth, an appetite greatly stimulated by the expanding circulation of goods and the new opportunities for profit that characterized the emergence of market economies. Thus the landowners of England did not accelerate the enclosure of the common lands at the end of the eighteenth century because they needed wage labor. Neither did the plantation owners of the American South evict sharecroppers in the middle of the twentieth century to secure laborers. To the contrary, the English agricultural population of the late eighteenth century had been increasing rapidly, and there was a surplus of workers. The common lands were enclosed to take advantage of the new opportunities for profit created by expanding markets for grains and wool, and by improvements in agricultural technology. Sharecroppers were thrust out of the plantation system in the American South because the mechanization of agriculture greatly reduced the need for hand labor. In these and other instances, the displacement of people from the traditional subsistence economy was merely the indifferent consequence of the search for profits. But whether the displacement of people from the pre-industrial community was the self-conscious aim of those who sought profits through increasing the supply of wage labor or merely the by-product of the search for profits through increased landownership or improved technology, the consequence was the same. It was the loss of subsistence resources that forced people into the labor market.

The new system intruded on the organic order of the traditional community slowly, and in different ways in different places. At first, features of what we now recognize as a labor market only modified traditional relations. As the English landowning aristocracy began to commercialize their holdings in the fourteenth and fifteenth centuries, many of the peasantry lost their rights to the land and became agricultural laborers. But the terms of their hire were still very much influenced by traditional feudal relations, and they also retained their rights to the forests and the commons. As the commercialization of agriculture intensified over the succeeding centuries, and as landowners turned from tillage to pasturage in response to the demand for wool and from subsistence crops to cereal grains in order to take advantage of the increased demand for food created by the growing cities, the terms of employment became more starkly market-oriented. Workers who had once been hired by the year came to be hired by the season or even by the day, and wages that had once been paid in grain came to be paid in cash. Yet aspects of feudal labor relations survived, even in the New World of the American colonies, where perhaps half of the early immigrants who had arrived as bonded servants ended their lives as tenant farmers. Many others, of course, came as slaves and ended their lives as slaves.

In early manufacturing, relations between owners and workers, as formerly between masters and journeymen, were guided by laws and customs that lent these relations much of the stability of the traditional community. Moreover, a good many artisans were also still peasants, growing enough food for subsistence to give them some protection from market relations. Thompson characterizes the weaver population of England in the eighteenth century, for example, as made up of diverse groups: some were self-employed; others were journeymen; and many others were small-holders who worked part-time at the loom while deriving some of their sustenance, as always, from the soil. As the cotton industry expanded at the end of the eighteenth century and as conditions in agriculture worsened through enclosure and population growth, these part-time weavers became full-time weavers; together with the self-employed weavers and the displaced agricultural workers who had turned to the loom, they came to be submerged in a more or less uniform class of "proletarian outworkers" (1963, p. 271).

Nor is it entirely correct to think that labor markets were the inevitable corollary of an emerging capitalism. In many places, as in England of the fourteenth and fifteenth centuries, the long-standing linkage between work, subsistence, and the resources for work was broken long before anything that looked like modern capitalism developed. In other parts of the world, capitalism arrived without labor markets. The cotton, tobacco, and sugar plantation owners of the American South and the Caribbean, and later the rubber plantation owners of Indonesia, were firmly linked to international capitalist markets, but they maintained a system of local labor relations that was essentially feudal. Nevertheless, and whatever the specific historical reasons that made it expedient, the market system for allocating human labor became dominant in the countries that were to become the leaders of world capitalism.

PEOPLE RESISTED THE developments that forced them into wage labor. They resisted the loss of the resources that had once yielded them subsistence. They protested when the common lands on which they had grazed their animals were enclosed by large landowners, or when they found themselves evicted from the land they had tilled by legal maneuvers they did not comprehend, or when their livestock was confiscated to pay their debts, or when their ancient rights to the use of the products of the forests and the streams were rescinded. They protested again when food prices rose beyond their means, or when new taxes, dues, and rents were imposed that further eroded the margin of survival. They burned and poached and vandalized the property of the encroaching landlords; they rioted and looted the granaries of the rich for the food they thought rightfully belonged to the poor; they tore down the houses of the offending merchants and magistrates; they smashed the machines in the alien factories; they petitioned their kings and their governors for redress; they took to the road in banditry; they appealed to their God in millenarian movements of wrenching anguish and fantastic hope; and sometimes they provided the shock troops of revolutionary movements that transformed their societies.

A good many analysts who have looked back on these episodes of popular resistance define them as irrational expressions of the tensions generated by economic change. Neil Smelser, for example, following in the influential tradition of Durkheim and Parsons, thinks of them as "symptoms of disturbance" (p. 225 *passim*). But they were much more than that. They were part of a great centuries-long movement in defense of ancient rights to subsistence, in defense of the complex rights to the forests and the commons and the local food supply that had guaranteed people resources for subsistence. It was a movement of political resistance to the incursions on the traditional community by the new forms of exclusive property, and by the new economic relations that we today understand as capitalism. Political resistance was possible because people believed that they had rights to the land they worked and to food at a fair price. They retained ideas about a social life in which the reciprocal rights and obligations of different classes had ensured subsistence. The landowners and manufacturers violated those rights and defaulted on their obligations by stealing subsistence resources. Political resistance was possible, in other words, because people had ideas about their world, and those ideas led them to think that what was happening to them was neither necessary nor just.

Political resistance was also possible because the disruption of the traditional community that fired the indignation of the poor released them somewhat from the restrictions of custom and hierarchy. At the same time, most people still lived sufficiently within the social network of the traditional order to retain the solidarity of village life. The crucial importance of social organization in undergirding peasant resistance was brought to the attention of contemporary analysts by the work of Eric J. Hobsbawm (1965) and Barrington Moore, Jr. It was their point that the solidarities of everyday life make it possible for people to react collectively when their world is threatened. We may add that the networks of the traditional order provided peasants with access to the groups they perceived as responsible for the violation of their subsistence rights—to the local landowners whose crops they burned or in whose forests they poached; to the merchants whose stores they looted; to the manufacturers whose machines they smashed.

Sometimes, in moments of pervasive societal upheaval, the peasantry did not lose. The lasting achievement of the French Revolution was that the peasantry gained land; and because they did, industrialization in France was impeded by lack of a supply of labor for more than a century. So long as their land and livelihood were secure, the French peasantry did not leave the countryside to enter urban labor markets. The Indians who followed Zapata in the Mexican Revolution also eventually won rights to the land, imprinted in the post-revolutionary constitution, which helped to protect their holdings until the recent flush of oil wealth and the aggrandizement it stimulated.

Most of the time, the peasantry lost. They did not lose because landowners were immune to burning and poaching and rioting. They lost because the usurpations of owners were regularly defended by the legal authority and the armed force of the state. It was the state that imposed increased taxes or enforced the payment of increased rents, and evicted or jailed those who could not pay the resulting debts. It was the state that made lawful the appropriation by landowners of the forests, streams, and commons, and imposed terrifying penalties on those who persisted in claiming the old rights to these resources. It was the state that freed serfs or emancipated sharecroppers only to leave them landless.

Everywhere men and women fought bitterly over the processes through which private property was wrested out of subsistence rights, and through which the market in human labor was created. They resisted openly when they could, they eluded and evaded when they could not. But in most places at most times, a protesting rural people were no match for the forces of law and order that regularly came to the aid of owners.

The history of the usurpation of subsistence rights reveals with absolute clarity that property is not, as we often seem to think, a natural condition that antedates the political process. Property is a political artifact, created by state law and maintained by state force. And if some men and women "own" the resources needed for the production of valued goods, while others do not, that is also not a first and natural condition. It is a political condition emanating from a relationship with the state. If the state creates what we mean by property at any given time, it also alters the forms and distribution of property to achieve diverse and changing purposes. In the course of the several centuries in which the modern labor market was forged, state power was used to alter the forms of property by eliminating the complex use rights on which the subsistence of the traditional community depended. It was only as these use rights were stamped out that what we now call private property —the exclusive right to the possession, use, and transfer of resources—emerged.

ONCE PEOPLE WERE forced into the wage-labor relationship, the result was a history of low wages, long hours, iron discipline, and killing working conditions. But the fact that people were made into wage workers does not account for those travails, for the new type of relationship created by labor markets was not in itself a relationship in which workers were powerless against owners. The relationship between owners and workers was in fact one of interdependence: those who owned property needed labor as much as those who labored needed the resources of the propertied to make their labor productive. If each needed the other, then each had leverage over the other. Employers could fire the people who needed employment to earn a subsistence, and so they had power over them; and workers could refuse to labor for the employers who needed labor to turn land or other resources to profit, and so they also had power.

But interdependence in principle was not interdependence in reality. State law and state power were again brought to bear on behalf of property in ways which ensured that employers could use the threat of withholding employment far more effectively than workers could use the threat of withholding labor. On the one side, the law left employers free to fire workers, to collude in setting wages low, and to conspire in seeing to it that dissident workers turned out of one job did not have an easy time finding another. On the other side, beginning in the sixteenth century, workers were bound by English law to work for any who wanted to hire them, and both English law and American colonial law fixed maximum wages and minimum hours. Collusion and "combination" by workers were declared illegal in England by legislative enactments beginning in the sixteenth century and culminating in the Combination Acts of 1779 and 1800. Until the mid-nineteenth century in the United States, the courts held that unions were criminal conspiracies; later, the Sherman Anti-Trust Act of 1890 provided the basis for declaring unions to be illegal combinations or conspiracies in restraint of trade. Even after the Clayton Anti-Trust Act of 1914 explicitly declared that unions were not illegal combinations in restraint of trade, striking workers were nevertheless, until the Great Depression, regularly subjected to court injunctions and criminal prosecutions, and to the coercive power of police and state militia.

Still, working people continued to resist domination within the wage-labor relationship. When they could not organize legally, they organized illegally, and often successfully, for the law could not easily penetrate the solidarities formed by closely knit work groups and working-class communities, as the histories of the Luddites and the organizations of American miners illustrate. When workers could not strike legally they struck illegally, as shown by the sheer volume of court injunctions issued in the United States. Even guns did not entirely quell resistance; otherwise the pages of American labor history would not be smeared with the blood of so many murdered strikers.

IT TOOK TWO other kinds of action by the state to enable capital to dominate labor. Just as state policies in the interests of property weakened workers in their overt struggles within the workplace, these additional measures further eroded the power of workers by altering the conditions of the labor market and adding to its terrors. One set of measures served to maintain high levels of unemployment, and the other to restrict the availability of public outdoor relief to the unemployed. In combination, these policies kept workers weak and wages down.

We have said that in principle workers and owners were interdependent; but the relative dependence of one upon the other varied, depending on which side needed the other more. When labor markets were tight, employers were the more vulnerable and wages rose. When labor markets were slack, it was workers who were the more vulnerable, for they could easily be replaced, and wages fell. In other words, large numbers of the unemployed were like large quantities of anything else in an unimpeded market: as the supply increased, the price fell, because, in the scramble to survive, people searching for work underbid both one another and those who were then working.

And the price of their labor often did fall. The spread of labor markets brought into being a phenomenon previously so uncommon it had not even acquired the name that was soon to become as familiar as the condition it described: unemployment. In the traditional community, work and subsistence had often been jeopardized by natural forces—by drought or blight, for example—and sometimes by war. But now work and subsistence were being made conditional on a set of forces that emanated not from nature but from a system of economic relations that some people had created and were imposing on other people. The spread of markets made the availability of work and subsistence radically uncertain, for work depended on employment, and employment depended on the state of the market.

When the market contracted or collapsed in the cyclical downturns that were to characterize capitalist economies, large numbers of workers became jobless at the same time, with a devastating effect on wage levels. Rapid shifts in markets often had the same effect, because these shifts meant that production expanded in some industries in some places and contracted in other industries in other places, with the result that large numbers of workers often found themselves in the wrong places or with the wrong skills. Thus, the new class of proletarian handloom weavers created by the expanding market for cotton at the end of the eighteenth century in England soon enlarged to constitute roughly one-third of the working population. But it was a class that was to be destroyed even more rapidly than it had been created, and by the same market forces that brought it into being. As the factory mode of production took hold in the nineteenth century, the supply of cotton increased rapidly, and the price fell. The handloom weavers could not compete with machines; nor could they compete with the low wages paid the women and children whom the factory owners preferred to hire. Earnings from the handloom dropped steadily, until the weavers were starved out of existence by a market that had rendered them superfluous.

Unemployment was not only the result of market vicissitudes. Because the supply of people needing jobs governed the terms of the labor-market relationship, employers manipulated that relationship by enlarging the pool of potential laborers. There was nothing exceptionally dark or unscrupulous about such efforts in the world of the market. Market actors always try to manipulate the supply of anything that affects their fortunes. Workers tried to manipulate the supply of labor as well, with exclusionary rules of various kinds that limited eligibility for employment. Employers, however, were far more successful, for they could draw upon the powers of the state.

In England, the first major effort by employers to control the labor market occurred in the fourteenth century, when feudal relations predominated but were weakening. The immediate precipitant was the Black Death of the years 1348–1349, which decimated the population. The resulting labor shortage was intensified by the growing demand for workers occasioned by the rise of the weaving trade and by the new opportunities for escaped serfs to join armies raised for war. Together, these conditions improved the bargaining position of workers in emerging market relations. In response, landowners secured the passage of the Statute of Laborers, which effectively prohibited workers from exploiting the potential leverage of these more favorable labor-market conditions. It was made illegal for unpropertied men and women, whether bonded or free, to refuse any offer of employment, or to demand more than a fixed wage, or to leave their town or village in search of better terms of labor (Chambliss).

The same strategies used to force people into the labor market in the first place by eliminating the possibility for traditional subsistence were also used to force more people into the labor market than were actually needed by employers. The wage workers of nineteenth-century England scrambled for employment in competition with a displaced agricultural work force and with displaced Irish peasants as well. In the United States, where a rapidly expanding economy created the possibility in principle of a tight labor market and greater leverage for workers, industrialists sent labor contractors to Europe and the Orient to recruit immigrants on a huge scale, virtually indenturing them in exchange for their passage, an arrangement legalized by the Contract Labor Law of 1864, which wrapped the policy of open immigration in the banner of freedom. With the beginnings of the internationalization of capitalist production in the twentieth century, these processes were replicated in the colonial world as well, often in more brutal form, with the ultimate result that workers in the mother countries began to find their power in the wage-labor relationship undermined by competition from the impoverished millions of the Third World.

THE CENTURIES-LONG process by which people were made into wage workers, and by which unemployment systematically weakened their power as workers, was closely linked to developments in charity and relief arrangements. In the preindustrial community, charity was governed by time-honored rules that the better-off share some of their riches with the less well-off, and especially when scarcity afflicted the community. The feudal lord was bound by custom to open his storehouses to his vassals when the crops failed; the landlords of Southeast Asia were bound to reduce the share of the crop they took in rent if the subsistence of the peasantry was imperiled (Scott). From the perspective of the well-off, such charity had diverse motives: honor in this world, salvation in the next, and perhaps most important, maintenance of the sense of reciprocity that bound hierarchical communities together and helped prevent rebellion. From the perspective of the poor, charity was a central component of the complex of subsistence rights that constituted what Thompson calls the "moral economy" of the traditional community (1971). But in the face of the break-up of old patterns of work and subsistence and the spread of wage labor, these age-old forms of charity came to be viewed by the propertied as less than honorable and less than godly.

One reason was that charity, like other subsistence rights, was an alternative to wage labor. Thus the fourteenth-century Statute of Laborers, which attempted to limit the bargaining power of workers by prohibiting their mobility and fixing their wages, also prohibited the giving of alms.

Because that many valiant beggars, as long as they may live of begging, do refuse to labour, giving themselves to idleness and vice, and sometimes to theft and other abominations; it is ordained, that none, upon pain of imprisonment shall, under the colour of pity or alms, give anything to such which may labour, or presume to favor them toward their desires; so that thereby they may be compelled to labour for their necessary living. [cited in Chambliss, p. 68]

As market relations supplanted traditional economic relations in the commercial centers of Northern Europe, preoccupation with the control of vagrancy and beggary grew. What had been a right in the traditional community—the right to seek alms—now became a crime. The penalties for the crime were elaborated and the punishments made ever more terrifying—the magistrates of Basel defined no less than twenty-five different categories of beggars, each with a prescribed punishment. By the sixteenth century in England, when labor market relations were rapidly spreading, the idle who could not give an account of how they earned their living were to be stripped naked, tied to the end of a cart in the market town, and beaten until bloody. Second offenders were to be whipped again and their right ear cut off. Third offenders were to be executed as felons. The elaboration of such rituals of terror was not capricious. Something important was at stake, and the propertied classes said clearly enough what it was. If the poor were allowed their traditional right to charity, they might evade wage labor.

But charity had also accomplished important purposes. It had helped bind the rich and poor together under one God, and it had also helped the poor to see that the rich served an actual function in the practical life of the subsistence community. In other words, the aid that the rich gave the poor mitigated class antagonisms. With the rise of market arrangements, some system of charity continued to be necessary,

particularly because the poor themselves still held to the old
moral economy, to the view that those in distress had a right
to aid by the will of God, and they often expressed such
convictions by rioting. Charity could not be altogether eliminated if peace was to be maintained. Yet charity, like other
subsistence resources, interfered with the efforts to force the
poor into wage labor. The danger of liberal charity was that the
subsistence it provided could become an alternative to the
backbreaking employment at low wages for which the poor
were wanted.

Landowners and kings, merchants and magistrates, all exerted themselves to contrive a solution. Out of this effort, a
new institution arose beginning in the early sixteenth century.
The new institution was designed to respond to the dual imperatives of enforcing wage labor while moderating the protests of
the poor. This new charity would not be haphazardly dispensed
by the wealthy or by the Church. It would be firmly under the
control of the state, and organized according to principles that
would guide it through the narrow shoals erected by the dual
imperatives that had prompted its invention.

In time, the new institution also acquired a name. It was
called poor relief. Relief, like charity, might be necessary for
social harmony, but it had to be administered strictly—strictly
enough to drive people from a disrupted subsistence economy
into the labor market, and strictly enough to ensure that they
would have little option but to accept employment on whatever terms were offered. In other words, relief policies were
important to the landowners, merchants, and early manufacturers of Europe and America because they impinged directly
on the basic conflict between the propertied and the propertyless over the new labor market arrangements, and the terms of
labor in the new market arrangements.

In response to these concerns, poor relief became an arena

for an extraordinary exercise of statecraft. A continuous stream of innovations and reforms evinced a deliberate and self-conscious effort to contrive a set of arrangements that would prevent the use of relief by the poor as an alternative to employment while still permitting sufficient relief to be given to maintain some appearance of reciprocity, of the sense that the rich had met their duties and the rights of the poor had been honored, and particularly in the face of riot and insurrection. Administrative inventions to achieve these dual ends proliferated, but two main principles emerged that guided the administration of relief for centuries and continue to guide the administration of programs to relieve the poor in our own time. One principle was simply to refuse aid to all who were deemed able-bodied and employable, no matter whether there was in fact available employment. Another was to make conditions for the receipt of aid so abhorrent and so shameful than even the harshest work was preferable. It was this latter principle that led, beginning in the eighteenth century, to the adoption of "indoor relief," or workhouses, in both England and the United States. Although often called "houses of industry," they were in reality houses of degradation, disease, and near-starvation.

But although the principles of relief policy that would effectively enforce wage labor were understood, the actual administration of relief in England and the United States remained relatively liberal until well into the nineteenth century, workhouses notwithstanding. Relief was dispensed to a good many people, usually in the less restrictive form of "outdoor relief." In a very general sense we can say that throughout this period the use of relief by elites to maintain a sense of reciprocity and harmony between the propertied and propertyless was more urgent than its use to enforce labor. However, that did not happen because elites were social analysts.

If the propertied understood the importance of relief and
made it the focus of their political energies, so did the poor.
And as long as the old ideas regarding subsistence rights remained vital, and as long as the poor retained enough of the
old pre-industrial solidarities to enable them to join together,
they were able to force the propertied to honor their ancient
right to charity, sometimes by petition, but more often by riot.
In other words, the propertied understood the importance of
social harmony and the uses of a liberal relief in maintaining
such harmony mainly because they were periodically compelled
to understand by insurrection. In the eighteenth century, English relief reformers repeatedly attempted to turn relief policy
more effectually to the task of enforcing wage labor by limiting
aid to the workhouse. But the poor tore down many of these
"houses of industry," demanding "that the poor should be
maintained as usual; that they should range at liberty and be
their own masters" (Webb and Webb, quoted in Tilly, p. 3).
Tilly reviews some of these events and concludes:

> Attacks on poorhouses, concerted resistance to enclosures,
> food riots, and a number of other common forms of eigh-
> teenth-century conflict all stated an implicit two-part theory:
> That the residents of a local community had a prior right to
> the resources produced by or contained within the commu-
> nity; that the community as such had a prior obligation to
> aid its weak and resourceless members. The right and the
> obligation should take priority over the interest of any partic-
> ular individual and over any interest outside the community.
> . . . That was, in E. P. Thompson's terms, the ill-articulated
> but powerful theory of the "moral economy." [pp. 3–4]

For over two centuries in England and the United States,
the poor were partially victorious. To be sure, they did not

succeed in halting the forces that were pre-empting their rights to the land and the forests, thus eliminating use rights and creating property rights. Still, their protests were sufficiently threatening to force the relatively liberal dispensation of poor relief, particularly in the wake of riots.

But in the longer run, the poor lost this struggle as well, conspicuously in the United States, where public relief was more or less abolished during the last third of the nineteenth century. Part of the reason for the total obliteration of the subsistence claims of the poor was that these claims, and the protests through which they were advanced, were overwhelmed by the strength and single mindedness of the new owning class that arose with industrial capitalism, a group that in the United States pursued its interests unfettered by any residual feudal notions of mutuality and reciprocity between classes. Moreover, during the emergence and rapid expansion of industrial capitalism, the new owning classes had priorities more urgent than maintaining social peace. Rapid industrial growth generated an intense need for an enlarged pool of wage labor, while the instabilities resulting from the ferocious competition of the period—as represented by the extreme and rapid fluctuations of the business cycle—drove industrial capitalists to reduce wage costs. This was accomplished in part, as we said earlier, by encouraging vastly increased immigration from abroad. (In England, where a comparable period of industrialization occurred some forty years earlier, a displaced agricultural work force provided the fodder for the expanding labor market.) Meanwhile, industrialists exerted themselves to intensify work discipline while reducing wages, in part by smashing organizations of skilled laborers and eliminating their supervisory role in the work process in favor of routinization and mechanization. None of this was accomplished easily. Strikes and riots spread in the late nineteenth century, as they had in

England in the early 1800s. And so did the use of police, militia, and troops to combat worker protests.

Not surprisingly, the abolition or slashing of outdoor relief was a central part of this mobilization by industrialists, for relief made it possible for some of the poor to evade the new industrial assault. Outdoor relief was eliminated in most of the big cities of the United States beginning in the 1870s, under the banner of the "scientific" philanthropy movement, which claimed that indiscriminate charity caused the problems of unemployment and poverty it was supposed to solve by indulging the character defects of the poor. An earlier and similar effort by the new manufacturing class in England resulted in the Poor Law reform of 1834, which was intended to abolish outdoor relief in favor of the workhouse. William Cobbett, the fiery journalist-hero of the English working class, defined this reform as the final and deepest violation of the ancient rights of the poor:

> Among these rights was . . . the right, in case we fell into distress, to have our wants sufficiently relieved out of the produce of the land, whether that distress arose from sickness, from decrepitude, from old age, or from inability to find employment. . . . For a thousand years, necessity was relieved out of the Tithes. When the Tithes were taken away . . . compensation was given in the rates as settled by the poor-law. The taking away those rates was to violate the agreement, which gave as much right to receive in case of need, relief out of the land, as it left the landowner a right to his rent. [cited in Thompson, 1963, p. 761]

Polanyi later remarked of the turn from outdoor to indoor relief in England, "Psychological torture was coolly advocated and smoothly put into practice by mild philanthropists as a means of oiling the wheels of the labor mill" (p. 82). His remarks apply as well to the abolition of outdoor relief in the United States. By the end of the nineteenth century, the American poor had lost even their residual right to poor relief, the terrible depressions of the period notwithstanding. They had thus been stripped of the last of their subsistence rights.

It is not difficult to understand the motives of industrial capitalists in undertaking this assault. They understood, as other men of property understood before them and after them, that poor relief stood as an obstacle to their efforts to enlarge the pool of wage labor and to intensify the exploitation of wage labor. Nineteenth-century capitalists understood, as twentieth-century capitalists also understand, the historical relationship between unemployment, wage levels, and relief.

STILL, THE CRUCIAL question remains unanswered. Why did the new industrial classes win out in the struggle over subsistence resources? Why were they able to shape government action to their own interests in ways that conceded nothing to popular resistance? We turn now to that question, for the answer bears on our general conclusion that they are unlikely to succeed again.

3

THE
WALLS
AROUND
DEMOCRACY

*B*Y THE CLOSE of the nineteenth century in the United States, property rights prevailed over subsistence rights. Most working people had become wage laborers. And within the wage-labor relationship, owners were dominant, not because of their economic power, but because of their political power. Government on all levels promulgated the laws and court decisions that declared illegal the exercise of worker power through strikes. And when the authority of the law was not sufficient, government provided the firepower that crushed strike power. Moreover, the political power of employers also enabled them to eliminate the right of the poor and the unemployed to poor relief. All of this mattered greatly. The state policies that supported property help account for the extraordinary rapidity of the growth of industrial capitalism in the

United States after the Civil War, while also suggesting an explanation for the uniquely dangerous and onerous conditions that prevailed in American factories, mines, and mills.

How was this virtually complete domination of state policy by business possible? The question is less compelling in the context of European development, where the various alliances of convenience between monarchy, landowners, and industrialists were articulated and reinforced within institutional arrangements that barred the mass of the populace from any form of political participation, short of riot and revolt, until the end of the nineteenth century. In any case, the dominance of business and industry in most European countries was never so complete; it was moderated at first by the influence of a feudal landowning class, and later by the power of industrial workers. The question is more compelling in the context of American development, for in the United States the franchise was widely distributed from the beginning of the republic, and whatever property qualifications had existed were eliminated in most states by the 1820s. White working men had the vote almost from the beginning of American political life. Why then did the democratization of politics leave the great majorities who were poor so powerless to deal with the urgent issues of their existence?

It will not do to dismiss the granting of procedural rights to participation in government as a mere sop extended to the mass of the population to distract them from the economic depredations that accompanied the spread of market relations. Indeed, European workingmen did not win the franchise easily or early precisely because the owning classes thought the wide distribution of the vote would jeopardize property. Never was the issue more clearly posed than during the debates at Putney within Cromwell's New Model Army in 1647 when democracy was only a vision, a vision evoked for common people when they joined a revolution that is generally understood to have been a revolution of the rising English bourgeoisie. The argument for universal male suffrage was stated by Colonel Rainborough, radical Leveller leader:

> For really I think that the poorest he that is in England hath a life to live, as the greatest he; and therefore truly, sir, I think it's clear, that every man that is to live under a government ought first by his own consent to put himself under that government.

And General Ireton, Cromwell's son-in-law, replied just as succinctly that mass political rights would endanger property rights:

> No person hath a right to an interest or share in the disposing of the affairs of the kingdom . . . that hath not a permanent fixed interest in this kingdom. . . . All the main thing that I speak for, is because I would have an eye to property. . . . If you admit any man that hath a breath and being, [a majority of the Commons might be elected who had no] local and permanent interest. Why may not these men vote against all property? . . . Show me what you will stop at; wherein you will fence any man in a property by this rule. [cited by E. P. Thompson, 1963, p. 22]

This answer echoes through history. Some two hundred years later, in the aftermath of the Third Reform Bill, the historian J. A. Froude warned of the meaning for property of the extension of the franchise in an address to the Liberty and Property Defense League in London:

> It is one man one vote. And as the poor and the ignorant are the majority, I think it is perfectly certain—and it is only

consistent with all one has ever heard or read of human nature—that those who have the power will use it to bring about what they consider to be a more equitable distribution of the good things of this world. [quoted by Brittan, p. 146]

These worries explain why the British ruling classes held fast against worker demands for democratic rights until the late nineteenth century. Not until the popular movement in defense of subsistence rights was stamped out, not until industry, empire, and wage labor were in place, did British workingmen gain the franchise.

Just as the propertied feared democracy because it would give the poor power against property, so the poor fought for democratic rights for the same reason. From the Levellers in the New Model Army in the seventeenth century, to the American mechanics and laborers in the Revolutionary period who demanded democratic rights in order to control prices, reduce taxes, and curb the accumulation of wealth, to the insurgent French workers of the nineteenth century who called for a "Democratic and Social Republic," ordinary people have always thought that formal political rights to participation would give them the power to force the state to act on their economic grievances.

With the usual advantage of historical hindsight, such ruling-class fears and working-class hopes appear unfounded, or at least greatly exaggerated. Neither the English nor any of the other enfranchised working-class men of Europe or the United States used the franchise when they gained it to vote "against all property." Yet there was an indisputable logic to the fear and to the hope, particularly during a period when the poor were being stripped by the propertied of their ancient subsistence rights and forced into the "wheels of the labor machine." If the poor were granted formal political rights, why would they not use the vote to resist these encroachments, and to resist effectively, since the transformation of working people into wage laborers was ultimately accomplished by state law and state force? And once this transition was completed and formal democratic rights were finally ceded, even then the anxiety of the ruling classes was not entirely without cause. To be sure, the political parties that formed to organize the votes of European workers did not rise up to challenge all property. But the franchise did offer workers some power in defending themselves against the propertied classes in wage-labor relations, as revealed by the moderation with which European governments came to deal with mass strikes, the comparative effectiveness of European state policies to reduce industrial and mining hazards, and the earlier adoption by most industrial European countries of health programs, old-age pensions, and unemployment insurance.

The great anomaly arises in the United States, for nowhere else did the working class have so little political power, and yet nowhere else were its formal rights so extensive at so early a stage of capitalist development. This is the puzzle that demands explanation. How was it possible for capital to triumph, and to triumph so fully, in the context of the most fully developed democratic laws in the world?

The men of property who set out to create a new government following the Revolutionary War were as apprehensive as their English counterparts about the threat to property posed by mass enfranchisement. But their situation was far more tenuous and unstable, and their ability to withhold the franchise commensurately weaker. They set out to build a nation-state in the aftermath of a revolution fought by the common people. The support of the farmers, artisans, and urban poor who made up the troops of the Revolutionary Army had been earned by the promise of the democratic idea, the most powerful idea of its time; moreover, these people were still insurgents, and still armed. Nor did the American men of property have the enormous advantage of an existing state apparatus with which to stamp out ideas and quell disorder. They were not shielded by the panoply of traditional authority of an established state, or by the monopoly of legitimate force of an established state. And a revolutionary elite could not, in the wake of an upheaval they had themselves incited, resist democratic demands by evoking respect for traditionalism itself, by claiming the authority born of the continuity of patterns of domination and subordination. As Governor Berkeley of Virginia had written a hundred years earlier, during Bacon's Rebellion, "How miserable that man is that Governs a People where six parts of seven at least are Poor Endebted Discontented and Armed" (Zinn, p. 40).

This was the dilemma that preoccupied those who would rule the new nation. Madison stated it clearly in the famous Federalist Paper Number Ten. Some kind of representative system was needed to maintain peace among the numerous factions in the new nation. But a representative system also posed dangers, for the factions to which Madison referred were not only those based on the numerous divisions of culture, region, or interest. The most serious and threatening factional division was that between the rich and the poor, the division generated by "the various and unequal distribution of property. Those who hold and those who are without property have ever formed distinct interests in society." The true danger, then, was not a "faction"; it was a majority without property, a majority that could use democratic rights against the propertied minority.

The seriousness with which the founders of the republic took this threat is suggested not only by their pontifications on the subject but by the elaborate institutional arrangements that they established in the nation-building period to limit the democratic capacities of the majority, while acknowledging and formalizing democratic rights within the structures they created. The wondrous intricacies that resulted are familiar: an elaborate arrangement of "checks and balances" in the national government, which was intended to check and balance what Hamilton called "the imprudence of democracy"; indirect elections for the most important offices on the state and federal level (where the presidency and the Senate were protected from popular election, and the Court was appointed); and the outright denial of the franchise to women, the unpropertied, blacks, and Indians, restrictions that were incorporated in most state constitutions adopted during the Revolution itself. These were not the only limitations on democratic rights, as we shall go on to note. They were merely the most obvious.

As it turned out, a number of these apparent limitations were short-lived, although some persisted and helped undergird a more enduring solution to the dilemma posed by democratic rights. From the Jacksonian period onward, the franchise was progressively extended. Virtually all white men had gained the vote by the 1820s; the elaborate electoral procedures that had shielded most officials from voters were eliminated, as elections were held more frequently and more and more key federal, state, and municipal officeholders were made to stand for direct election. Moreover, this extension of democratic rights took place without much resistance from elites or much turmoil from below.

One reason for the ready ceding of expanded democratic rights was the rapid proliferation of techniques for coercing votes and manipulating voting results. Coercion took different forms, including brute force. Its most pervasive form, however, was almost surely the use of a range of sanctions, short of force, to coerce people in their voting choices. These sanctions were as varied as the range of government powers that bore on the daily life of people. The authority to levy taxes, distribute charity, and imprison debtors could be used selectively to punish and reward. As time went on, government powers multiplied. Many occupational activities became subject to licensing; housing, sanitation, and construction were regulated by codes. And with each increment to governmental authority, the possibilities for the use of political discretion to reward and punish were augmented. Moreover, whether or not people acquiesced in the face of these threats, American electoral practices were rife with fraud. Voter-registration procedures kept "unreliable" groups from voting; gerrymandering distorted and weighted voting results; and when these formal arrangements were not sufficient, there were the colorful machine practices, which ranged from stuffing ballot boxes to posting thugs at voting booths. Such practices altered the political behavior of Americans and no doubt also weakened faith in the efficacy of democratic rights.

That substantial coercion and fraud characterized the American political past is indisputable. We know something of its significance in containing protest movements. But we do not know how pervasive it was in "normal" or electoral politics, and neither does anyone else. It is a large question, and it will not be clarified until political historians turn from studying voting results to scrutinizing more closely and systematically the conditions under which those results were produced.

Although the possibility exists that coercion and fraud were sufficiently widespread to prevent the emergence of electoral challenges or to preclude their success, that is not likely. Democratic rights were limited and twisted by coercion and fraud, but they were not nullified, for electoral challenges did occur, and they failed for lack of popular support. Another and ultimately more powerful solution to the challenge posed by democratic rights had emerged, and it was to shape American politics until our own time.

LAISSEZ-FAIRE IDEAS provided the more enduring solution to the democratic dilemma. In the world portrayed by this doctrine, the economic and political realms were separate, as if these realms were autonomous in the true and natural order of things. The economic relationships that evolved with the rise of capitalism were defined as the products of nature, not as the products of action by men and women. Just as nature was governed by inviolable laws, so too were economic activities governed by inviolable market laws. If these laws were permitted to operate freely, the economic activities of rational and self-seeking individuals would yield the twin blessings of prosperity and social harmony. Indeed, market laws came to displace the primacy of the laws of nature, for the latter were never given such awesome due. And if, as a concomitant result of the operation of market laws, many were left desperately poor while others became fabulously rich, this too redounded to the greater good. Poverty and riches were evidence, not of injustice, but of the fact that the market and its unerring laws had duly punished the slothful and untalented while rewarding the industrious and meritorious.

The vigor of this ideology in Europe, as others have noted, was sustained by the service it gave a capitalist class struggling to break loose on the one side from a mercantilist alliance with the crown and on the other side from a landed feudal class. These late-eighteenth- and nineteenth-century ideas justified the emancipation of the bourgeoisie both from economic regulations by the absolutist state and from persisting feudal constraints. The emerging capitalist class was ready to have done with state monopolies, restraints on trade, and regulations governing prices and labor. This was a battle undertaken in the name of freedom, the freeing of property from the fetters imposed by state and custom. Accordingly, property rights came to be viewed as the very bedrock on which all other liberties depended.

The emancipation of property from the tyranny of the state did not, however, free ordinary people from the tyranny of property or from the tyranny of state action taken in defense of property. The banner of liberty unfurled by the bourgeoisie was meant to fly over property, not over people. The historical context that produced *laissez-faire* ideology was thus as much political as it was economic, for the bourgeoisie was demanding new state economic policies in the name of liberty.

In the United States, the climactic moment of bourgeois liberation occurred simultaneously with the challenge of popular democracy. Having liberated itself from the English crown and English mercantile domination, the American elite had also to deal with an armed population fired by the democratic ideal. The important point about *laissez-faire* ideology for our purposes is thus neither its characterization of economic life nor its role in justifying the political ascendance of a capitalist class. The important point is the implications of this ideology for popular politics.

In treating the market as governed by "laws," *laissez-faire* ideology argued that economic relationships could brook no interference by government, except on penalty of inhibiting the market processes that generated wealth and perhaps on penalty of creating economic disaster. Economic issues were defined as properly beyond the reach of the state, and therefore beyond the reach of democratic majorities that participated in the state. In the fully developed form they acquired in the United States, these ideas made economic questions unthinkable as a matter of politics, surely an amazing feat.

It was all the more amazing that these ideas could triumph in the nineteenth century, for the concept of the economic and political as separate was wholly new. It departed entirely from the traditional community, where political and economic roles and relationships had not been separated, in actuality or in ideology. The prince's revenues came from his estates, where he was both landlord and ruler, the peasant both tenant and subject, and the rents owed by the peasant to the landlord were also the dues owed to the ruler. In such a world, most of what is usually meant when we speak of political rights—the right to speak freely, to assemble, to vote—did not exist. The main political rights of common people pertained to their economic situation, to their struggle for subsistence. Their justifiable claims on political authority had to do with their right to use the land or the forest, or to ply a particular trade, or to buy bread and grain at a fair price, or to receive sustenance in times of distress. The significance of the new doctrine of separation, which arose at the historical moment when the idea of democratic rights first captured the popular mind, is that these subsistence rights were then lost.

It has often been said that the American experience is distinctive because it developed in the absence of a feudal past. The American mind was, so to speak, uncluttered by an ideological heritage that defined a world of bounded classes governed by reciprocal rights and duties. Lockean liberal philosophy could thus presumably have taken deep root. This is only the most popular of a number of arguments purporting to explain why American workers lacked the class consciousness of European workers, arguments that are often grouped together as theories of "American exceptionalism" (although some theorists view the absence of class issues as the glory of American politics, and others think the reverse).*

*Other theories of exceptionalism emphasize opportunities for mobility, or the importance of racial and ethnic divisions, or the early distribution of the franchise, in accounting for the absence of class consciousness in the

Of the various exceptionalist perspectives, the view that the vigor of *laissez-faire* ideology in America had something to do with the rupture from feudal Europe strikes us as the most directly pertinent to our inquiry. The argument is more convincing, however, when it is slightly recast. Perhaps the destruction of old concepts of economic rights and the promulgation of the new doctrine of the separateness of the political realm were facilitated in the United States less because it lacked a feudal past than because it lacked a feudal present. In Europe, market relations evolved in the context of still-existing feudal relationships and still-existing feudal classes. In the

United States. We do not mean to choose among these arguments, most of which Katznelson (1980) has cogently summarized and evaluated. Unlike Katznelson, we think they are possibly all partly true, and they have some bearing on our argument. Opportunities for mobility were, at least until the mid-nineteenth century, almost surely greater in the United States than in Europe (Gutman), and there were also free land and free mining in the West, at least for those who were not destitute. The significance of such opportunities was probably less in the numbers that they actually enabled to advance than in their effectiveness in sustaining the hope of mobility among those left behind. The prospect of mobility diluted class consciousness, this variant of exceptionalism asserts, by suggesting that upward advancement was a solution to felt problems. Thus the belief in individual advancement may have helped ward off challenges to the doctrine of the separation of economic and political life. It is also true that American workers were divided by race and ethnicity, although as Gutman, Aronowitz, and Greenstone have each pointed out, strong ethnic and racial communities also nurtured class consciousness among their own members. But perhaps a working class fragmented by multiple divisions could not so easily see the mobilization of political majorities as a means of dealing with economic problems. Bendix is probably also right when he says, following T. H. Marshall, that the wide ceding of the franchise before the wrenching industrial transformation took place promoted a sense of participation among working people. In its more general form this argument asserts that people were deterred from challenging economic inequalities precisely because they were granted political equality. Capitalism was thus protected by the granting of democratic rights. This sort of explanation, however, leads back to the question we have been asking: Why did democratic rights prove effective in diluting the class consciousness of workers, or in legitimating economic inequalities, even while they proved ineffective in pressing working-class interests?

United States, however, many people owned the land they worked, although they were often deeply in debt, and others were artisans and laborers. True, these people had European origins, and in that sense they reflected a feudal history. But memories fade more quickly when there are fewer reminders in present experience, making the acceptance of entirely new ideas easier.

Still, this could not have been the whole story. If feudal ideas were reduced to remnants in the absence of a system of feudal relations to give them life, a similar discrepancy existed between emerging *laissez-faire* ideas and the developing American reality. From the very outset, the American economy was dependent on government policies, and so economic life was not being separated from politics at all. The doctrine of separation was an ideology in the old-fashioned sense of that term— in the sense of ideas that conceal rather than reveal social reality.

Thus from the beginnings of the American government in the late eighteenth century, policies were framed with "an eye to property." The merchants, bankers, and landowners who gathered at Philadelphia to write a constitution had become nation-builders precisely because they wanted national policies to protect and enhance their property. From this point of view, the writing of the Constitution was a bold ploy to promote trade among the colonies and to protect lenders, landowners, and shipping interests. Provisions for the establishment of a national currency, as well as those prohibiting the states from enacting laws creating trade barriers or impairing the obligation of contract, were intended to facilitate business dealings among the former colonies. The establishment of a national currency also precluded state legislatures from issuing cheap money in response to the demands of indebted farmers, as had happened in Rhode Island, thus securing the interests of bankers. The powers given the Congress to tax and spend were also bankers' measures, and they were of particular urgency to the gentlemen who convened in Philadelphia because most of them held bonds issued by the wartime Continental Congress that were in jeopardy. The large landholdings of this elite were made secure by the establishment of a standing army, as their shipping interests were secured by a navy. (And the powers ceded to the new government were rapidly employed after ratification to pass tariff laws to protect American merchants and manufacturers from European competition, and to impose new taxes to pay off the holders of war bonds.)

These were indisputably economic interventions by government. They were part of the framework of government policy without which a large-scale market economy cannot exist. And in the course of the nineteenth century, as the American market economy changed and expanded, yet other state policies were required or demanded by a changing and expanding propertied class. Thus the infrastructure of canals developed in the first half of the nineteenth century was financed by government; later the construction of a railway system was financed several times over by the enormous land giveaways and subsidies received by the railroad companies from federal, state, and local governments. More profits were made by trafficking in federal government bonds, through fraudulent wartime contracts, and from profitable traction and utility franchises granted by state and municipal governments. Meanwhile, the laws defining and protecting property were elaborated by state governments to create a new entity, the corporation, a legal fiction that protected entrepreneurs from personal liability for their failed business investments. Later, an interpretation by the Supreme Court gave this new entity the same rights enjoyed by persons under the due process clause of the Fourteenth Amendment. This curious argument permitted the

Court to nullify a number of state laws regulating railroad rates on the ground that the railroad corporations had been deprived of property without due process, and thus to erect a new line of constitutional defense against political interference with property. And as the nineteenth century wore on and industrial capitalism grew and flexed its muscles, the courts served it willingly in yet other ways. Contract law came to be interpreted so that workers could be virtually bonded to employers; the law of eminent domain permitted the appropriation of farms, homes, and small businesses for the construction of canals and railroads (and much later for highways and urban renewal projects). Mayors, governors, and presidents sent police, militia, and troops to break strikes, while the courts cooperated by enjoining strikers, by declaring unions to be in violation of antitrust laws, and sometimes by helping "frame" labor organizers as well. At the end of the century, as American industry flourished and its leaders began to look overseas for cheap resources and new markets, government obliged again by sending troops to make the United States an imperial power in Latin America and the Pacific.

In offering this familiar recapitulation, we merely repeat our earlier assertions—that the evolution of capitalist forms of property and the dominant position of the propertied in labor-market relations were made possible by the state and therefore by means of politics. And familiar though it may be, this recitation does serve to highlight the question with which we began: How was it possible for capital to triumph, and to triumph so fully, in the context of the most completely developed democratic arrangements in the world? We have given part of the answer: The political ascendance of capital was made possible by a doctrine that was so successfully translated into popular ideology that people were led to treat economic life and economic conflict as if they were distinct from politics.

Still, that ideology was at such variance with the reality of a history of state intervention on behalf of capital, and against ordinary people, that its vigor and persistence remain to be explained.

No IDEOLOGY CAN BE communicated and imposed by words alone. The interpretations people make of the world around them are, to be sure, influenced by the ideas that dominant classes propagate. Even so, people do not merely believe what they are told to believe. Ideas take root only if they are consistent with social life as people experience it, and they can be sustained only if they continue to be confirmed by social experience. Ideology, in other words, is bound up with structure, an insight that is one of the great contributions of Marxist thought. How, then, did a doctrine whose prescriptions were so at odds with the pattern of collusion between state and property come to have such force and durability?

The experience that nourishes ideology is itself a social construction. We shall argue that the experience of politics available to most Americans was organized by particular and elaborate institutional arrangements that concealed the alliance of state and property while simultaneously creating a concrete and visible arena of politics in which democratic rights mattered. Even as the economic activities of government on behalf of property were rendered almost invisible, other activities of government became the arena for a virtual festival of popular participation. The ideology of separation seemed credible, in short, because the institutions that organized American politics made it credible.

One such institutional arrangement was constitutionalism itself. If the men of property, when setting out to construct the new nation, had an "eye to property," the keenness of their eye must have been sharpened by the popular discontent and tu-mult of their time. A good deal of that discontent was, as we might expect, about economic issues: about confiscatory taxes, inflated food prices, and land evictions. There were price riots, the pulling down of the houses of the rich, and, especially, armed resistance to eviction by tenant farmers. Zinn reminds us of the thousands of small farmers, squatters, and tenants who, calling themselves "poor Industrious peasants," joined in the Regulator movement in North Carolina in the 1760s to denounce the "unequal chances of the poor and the weak . . . in contention with the rich and powerful" and to arm themselves to resist taxes, debt collection, and the confiscation of the property of tax delinquents (pp. 63–65). In New Jersey, Vermont, and New York, tenant farmers also took up arms repeatedly in protest against evictions by large landholders (and many sided with the British during the Revolutionary War for the good reason that their landlords supported the Revolution). And even while the post-Revolutionary elite were convening to debate the structure of a new national government, insurgent farmers, artisans, and laborers in Massachusetts, led by Daniel Shays, were rising in open rebellion against the tax collectors and sheriffs who were attempting to evict them from their land.

The new Constitution was intended to defend the proper-tied against these popular demands, not only by countering them with specific measures that precluded the immediate success of the insurgents, but by embedding these measures in the basic legal structure of the nation. Of course, phrases inserted into the Constitution are not irrevocable, and they are not always taken to mean what the Founders intended them to mean. As we know, the Constitution was bent in time to serve changing political purposes. But the bending of the Con-stitution was itself protected from popular influences by the constitutionally defined procedures for interpreting the Constitution. These procedures gave ultimate authority in determining the meaning of the Constitution to judges who were shielded from electoral influence by lifetime appointments. The accumulating decisions of the Court protected the changing forms of property from government interference in response to popular pressures. But the nine men who ultimately made these decisions claimed merely to interpret what had always been intended, what had been laid down by the Founding Fathers themselves. More than that, the constitutional procedures for amending the Constitution were cumbersome and difficult, and extremely unlikely to succeed in the face of opposition, even the opposition of a minority of the wealthy. Property was thus doubly shielded from what Hamilton had said were the "turbulent and changing" masses of the people who "seldom judge or determine right." Or, as Beard concluded in his well-known study, "The Constitution was . . . based upon the concept that the fundamental private rights of property are anterior to government and morally beyond the reach of popular majorities" (p. 324).

Of course, the Constitution also secured certain popular political rights against state interference. (It is well to remember that most of these rights were contained in the Bill of Rights, which was appended only as an expedient by the post-Revolutionary elite when they encountered opposition to ratification of the Constitution in some of the states.) But the equal standing of the constitutional protection of property from government interference and the constitutional protection of the exercise of political rights from government interference was deceptive. The meaning of political rights—to speak freely, to assemble, to petition, and to vote—was not only that these activities were protected by government. They also presumably guaranteed a way of exercising influence over government. If, however, government was in turn blocked from acting against property, then political rights could not become the vehicle to bring about effective state action on economic grievances. In this crucial area, political rights were thus constitutionally precluded from effective expression.

Moreover, to the extent that the right to speak freely or to assemble or to bear arms might have enlarged the capacities of workers and farmers in purely market struggles with property —in strikes and boycotts, for example—these rights were not in fact honored. Not until the twentieth century did the federal courts rule that the state governments were bound by the First Amendment, and private employers were never so bound. Employers were free to fire and blacklist employees who exercised these rights, and sometimes even to beat or kill them in the name of property rights. This is not to say that political rights were unimportant in American history. They were important, for they occasionally protected people who spoke out against the state itself, and they helped inspire the activism that characterizes American political culture. More than that, we will go on to argue that political rights did ultimately become a weapon against property rights. But that anticipates our analysis of the current conflict between capital and labor over the subsistence rights won through politics in the twentieth century. In the meantime, and for a long time to come, political rights were no match for property rights in any constitutionally determined contest.

Our point is not simply that these legal arrangements protected property against democratic influences. These protections were embedded in constitutionalism, and because they were, the sanctity of property came to be taken for granted— regarded as a first premise of the new polity rather than as an issue to be continuously debated and reconsidered. And because the protection of property constituted a fundamental structural element of the new polity, it became difficult to perceive these arrangements as contrived by some men in their efforts to dominate other men, and women. A judicial tradition that gave constitutional protections to property thus defined the true and natural boundaries of the political world; it was as if these boundaries represented another species of natural law, linked to and supporting the natural law of the market.

OTHER INSTITUTIONAL ARRANGEMENTS that stemmed from the legal structure created by the Constitution, but whose full realization was not determined by the Constitution, were also important in breathing life into the doctrine that insulated economic life from politics and government. One was the creation of a national government with powers that overarched the powers of town and state governments. The immediate impetus for the creation of a national government in the 1780s seems clear. The threatening mobilizations by the unpropertied were naturally enough occurring in the localities, although the reverberations reached and influenced state governments as well. The political action of ordinary people had always of necessity been local, for their ability to communicate and act was bounded by the organization of their everyday life on the farms and in the towns. The wealthy, by contrast, were linked to one another across great distances by their businesses and social networks. Thus the Founding Fathers had little difficulty organizing support among elites up and down the seaboard for the rapid ratification of the Constitution (which the Continental Congress had in fact never mandated them to write). They could travel and communicate with one another, if somewhat clumsily by modern standards. But for ordinary people at that time the communication of ideas and the organization of action on a national scale must have seemed inconceivable. A national government was, in short, a government that would be less influenced by popular opinion if only because of its inaccessibility to most people and its accessibility to some people.

This insight also helps explain the variable pattern of centralization and decentralization of policy that has marked American political history.* Despite a tendency for centralization through the growth of federal power, there nevertheless appears at first glance to be a certain randomness in the pattern of centralization and decentralization of particular policies. Underlying these stops and starts and reversals in the pattern of centralization, however, there were two overall historical tendencies. One was the tendency toward centralization of the policies critical to property, whether at the state or the national level, particularly as these policies were jeopardized by popular political mobilizations at the local level. When the business-oriented municipal reform movement was repeatedly defeated at the local level in the late nineteenth and early twentieth centuries, business interests simply shifted their attention to the state capitals, where they used their power to force reforms on resistant municipal governments; they also secured many other policies they wanted from state governments directly. Similarly, in the Progressive period, when statewide popular mobilizations directed at corporations threatened to result in state legislation that would restrict corporate dealings, as Kolko informs us, corporate leaders went to Washington to promote regulatory legislation of their own, framing the new proposals and regulations to soothe popular outrage while not impeding the flow of corporate profits. The significance of this centralizing tendency is that it made the business-oriented activities of

*The arguments that follow in this chapter draw in part on work done in collaboration with Roger Friedland and Robert Alford. See Friedland, Piven, and Alford; and Piven and Friedland.

government less visible and less accessible to popular influence. This was simply because, at least before the development of popular communication networks, the activities of state and national governments were less visible and less accessible.

But there was another and opposite historical tendency at work that contributed to the apparent randomness of patterns of centralization and decentralization. Even while many of the economic policies of the state were centralized, other policies less critical to property remained decentralized (and in our time are being deliberately localized, as can be seen in Nixon's effort to "return power to the people" in the form of revenue sharing, and Reagan's effort to do the same with block grants). Local government was vigorous in the United States in comparison with other Western countries, and its vigor resulted from the fact that localities did indeed do many things. They raised school taxes and property taxes, administered local schools, organized neighborhood services, and policed the streets. These were visible activities and the officials who administered them were accessible. The localization of these sorts of public activities made possible a vigorous and intense local politics—a school politics and a property-tax politics and a stoplight politics, as well as a politics of the patronage related to such activities. In other words, there was a level and there was a realm of government in which democratic rights mattered, but it was a different level and a different realm than that in which policies to protect and promote property figured largely. The variable centralization and decentralization of government policies, by thus stratifying the politics of property and the politics of democratic rights, helped give credibility to the doctrine that politics had nothing to do with economic matters.

But even within its own realm, local government was not in fact autonomous. Local governments acted, and local politics were played out, within larger institutional constraints that delimited the issues that could arise in school politics or property-tax politics or patronage politics. One set of constraints followed from the fact that local governments acted within limitations set by the policies of the federal and especially the state governments. Indeed, by the turn of the century, even such intensely local matters as public school policies had come to be framed and limited by both state education laws and private education organizations (funded by the wealthy), which promulgated influential national standards for curriculum, personnel, and school organization. More important, federal and state policies oriented to property helped form the very social and economic environment of local politics. Indeed, from the building of the canals to the financing of the railroads and then the highways, such policies helped to form or shatter the very cities and towns within which local politics occurred. But these constraints, like the state and federal policies that created them, remained in the background, always the framework but rarely the subject of the carnival and conflict of local politics.

There is another and less apparent sense in which the popular politics of the locality was constrained by the politics of property. One fundamental feature of the American polity is that it is what Schumpeter calls a "tax-state" (1954). He means simply that the state depends for revenue on the taxation of resources it does not itself control. The tax-state is like all states in that it has a natural interest in increasing the economic prosperity of its domain, both because prosperity makes possible the tax revenue upon which state power depends and because prosperity has everything to do with the domestic stability upon which rule depends. In these respects, the officials of the tax-state are no different from the feudal lords and absolute monarchs of Europe, who also had an interest in the prosperity and peace of the realm, and particularly in the prosperity of their estates and monopolies that were a source of revenue to maintain military and political power.

But the tax-state differs from other states because it must depend for prosperity, and for the revenues and tranquillity offered by prosperity, on resources it does not control. This is significant because the privatization of property also creates the potential for conflict between the state and the owners of property, despite their mutual interest in prosperity.

For the state, prosperity provides resources for the expansion of military power, as well as the conditions that ensure domestic peace. The propertied may also be interested in military expansion and domestic peace, but such interests are subordinate to the protection and increase of property. The kings of France, for example, became indebted to their bourgeois financiers because they needed money to pay for foreign wars. Naturally enough, the financiers were more interested in profit than in national greatness, and they deserted the monarchy when their loans were put in jeopardy. The state has interests of its own, and property has interests of its own. Their interests are complementary much of the time, particularly when, as in monarchical France and England, and in the United States for much of its history, state revenue could be extracted mainly by regressive taxation on the peasantry and on the goods consumed by working people. But when, in the interests of state power or domestic tranquillity, the state attempts to tax property, or to deny it the policies it demands, then its interests diverge, and the structure of the tax-state may offer property great political leverage (see Piven and Friedland).

Just how much leverage property can exert on the state depends on whether specific political and economic conditions permit the propertied to threaten the prosperity of the realm, thus jeopardizing both state revenues and political stability. One such condition is the relative mobility of property vis-à-vis the territorially bounded state. When property takes the form of land or natural resources, it is less mobile and therefore has less leverage over the state. Property in the form of capital may be quite mobile, however, and has greater leverage. Its mobility depends in turn on the territorial range of markets for the production and circulation of goods. In an international capitalist economy, Fred Block says, "If state managers pursue policies that large sections of the capitalist class see as posing serious challenges to their property rights, the results are likely to be a collapse of [investor] confidence . . ." (p. 9). In other words, when capital is mobile, it can withdraw investment. It can go on strike.

In the United States, the revenue dependence of government did not give capital a large source of power over the national government until after the Second World War. By then, the revenue requirements of the federal government had greatly enlarged, and American capital had begun to operate in international markets on a significant scale. Only under these conditions did the threat of disinvestment become real. Long before that, however, American capital operated in a national market and could thus exert substantial leverage over state and local governments. The legal protections guaranteed to property and the mobility afforded capital by a large-scale national economy combined to make decentralized government structures acutely vulnerable to the threat of disinvestment or to the promise of investment; businessmen could play off city against city, state against state. Thus when workmen's compensation laws were introduced into state legislatures early in the twentieth century, at a time of great popular indignation over killing and crippling industrial conditions, state political leaders feared that imposing taxes would drive manufacturing investment to other states. In the end, these laws were enacted only when manufacturing interests themselves combined in support of compensation laws, the better to ensure that compensation would be modest while precluding the prospect of proliferating damage suits (Lubove). The institutional arrangements that gave industry such great leverage over the state and local governments in which popular political participation was concentrated were, of course, an expression of politics. But it was a politics of structure rather than of policy, so that none of this appeared to be in the realm of politics at all.

Other institutional arrangements were also important in breathing life into the doctrine that severed politics from economic life. The American electoral system was organized in terms of territorial representation. People voted for representatives of precincts, wards, districts, and states. This sort of system tends to inhibit the emergence of economic issues when such issues are divisive, and can generate contention among the voters of a given territory. Parties and candidates search instead for the unifying issues more likely to bring together majorities within a given district. And in a vast country, where differences between regions and cultures are great, such territorial issues are not hard to find. Thus, on those occasions when economic issues did emerge in American politics, they tended to unite the people of one region against the people of another region, as the issue of "free silver" united the West against the East, or the issue of slavery united the North against the South.

But territorial issues were also prominent on the local level, as neighborhoods competed with each other for municipal patronage or municipal services. This was not simply because of territorial representation, for virtually all electoral representative systems are organized territorially. Another American political institution, built on the territorial system, was probably more important in suppressing economic issues. That institution was the political machine.

The wide extension of voting rights and the availability of

patronage from decentralized local governments, combined with a system of territorial electoral representation, helped create circumstances favorable to the development in nineteenth-century American cities of pervasive cliental relations between working people and the political system. Shefter explains that a series of reforms during the Jacksonian period facilitated this development, for the reforms freed the bureaucracies from the control of traditional social elites and thus made patronage available to party organizations. When workingmen's parties made up mainly of artisans began to form in the wake of the expansion of the franchise, some concessions were made in response to their demands, particularly in cities like New York and Philadelphia, where the workingmen were relatively strong. But that was not the whole of it. In New York, leaders of the party were quickly inducted into Tammany, and this early strategy suggested a method for creating a political organization that included working people while excluding their interests. As we said in an earlier study of the labor movement:

> Big city machines were able to win and hold the allegiance of workers by absorbing their leaders and by conferring favors and symbols that sustained the loyalties of workers on individual, neighborhood, and ethnic bases. This not only prevented the emergence of industrial workers as a political force directed to class issues, but it actually freed political leaders on all levels of government to use police, militia, and troops against striking workers without jeopardizing working-class electoral support. [1977, p. 106]

Ira Katznelson, in seeking to account for the absence of class issues in American urban politics, argues along parallel lines. American working people brought little class consciousness to local politics, he says, because the politics of work had been separated from the politics of community. The political machine figured largely in the blurring of class consciousness because it used patronage to organize "workers not as workers, but as residents of this or that ward, as members of this or that ethnic group." Katznelson continues:

> Although throughout the antebellum period such class-related economic issues as banking, tariffs, internal improvements, and slavery dominated the national and state political agendas, votes were increasingly solicited on the basis of ethnic and religious affiliations. It is striking that in a society undergoing very rapid change, and offering many possible points of conflict between groups and classes, the party system exploited locality-based ethnic divisions in the older cities more than anything else. [p. 61]

However, a politics of favors and symbols doled out to sustain individual, ethnic, and neighborhood political loyalties was only the public face of the machine. Most patronage was neither so visible nor so benign. The control of the votes of the mostly immigrant wards enabled the machine to win political offices. But the authority of those offices was used in another, far more private and important patronage exchange with business. It was the graft proffered by the traction, utility, insurance, and banking firms in return for the franchises, contracts, and interest-free deposits of nineteenth-century municipalities that greased the wheels of the political machine. The achievement of the machine, then, was its ability to nurture a politics of individualism, ethnicity, and neighborhood among working people, even while sustaining in another and hidden sphere the big-time politics of big-time profit.

The exceptional vitality of machine politics in the United

States was itself encouraged by the unusual degree of decentralization that characterized the American state structure. Decentralization provided a fertile ground for the development of
cliental relations, for it yielded the patronage that made possible the rapid growth of machines in the immigrant wards
without the need to capture a central state bureaucracy. Finally, a decentralized state structure also provided protected
enclaves within which the machine could weather attempts to
dislodge it.

The machine ultimately collapsed, undermined by decades
of reform maneuvers by the large numbers of businessmen who
were not profiting from franchises or municipal contracts and
who resented the high taxes the machine exacted and the
erratic public services it provided. Even before the machine
collapsed, however, these businessmen reformers were creating
new structural arrangements to take its place in insulating the
politics of property from popular politics. Because the machine
was so firmly lodged in the big cities, the reform effort often
took the form of locating the municipal functions that were
critical to business interests in separate agencies protected
from machine influence. The result was commissions, boards,
and authorities with mandated powers, for example, to control
capital infrastructure investments in such areas as transportation and construction. This pattern was not restricted to the
local level of government, for similar structures were created at
the state, regional, and federal levels in an expanding range of
policy areas, from the control of the money supply to the
regulation of communications. But the pattern was most pro-
nounced at the local level, for it was there that popular politics
was the most vigorous.

The administrative formula through which the bureaucratic
separation and insulation of policies critical to property was
accomplished is familiar. Agencies charged with such policies

were legally insulated from elected officials and the general public. Their officials were appointed, not elected, and appointees were often chosen from lists drawn up by business-oriented civic groups. Once appointed, these officials typically were secured by law against political removal. Procedures for public review of agency activities were minimal; the agencies were internally organized so that decision making was centralized, and they were otherwise made inaccessible to the public. All of this was usually justified on the ground that the governmental activities at issue were technical rather than political. Consistently, these agencies cultivated an elaborately specialized language and procedure that both exaggerated and justified their insulation and gave their activities the appearance of being matters fit only for experts, not politicians, to decide.

These reforms were put forward with unabashed self-righteousness; no less a commentator than Schumpeter insisted it was necessary for the very success of democracy that "the range of political decision should not be extended too far." But this constriction on politics, on democratic participation, should not be understood as a corresponding limitation on the power of the state. The Bank of England and the Interstate Commerce Commission in the United States, to use Schumpeter's examples, had to be insulated from politics precisely because such agencies were charged with crucial and complex matters that required the judgment of experts: on such matters, he was certain, "popular slogans . . . are almost invariably wrong" (1975, p. 292).

Whatever the policy rationale justifying the fragmentation of government, the political effect of locating some activities oriented to property in separate and bureaucratically shielded commissions and authorities, where they were then enveloped in a cloud of technical jargon, was again to render the politics of property less visible, at least as politics. Even to the extent that there was public awareness of what agencies such as the Federal Reserve Bank and the commercial banks with which it was allied did on the national level, or what agencies such as the New York Port Authority and the banks and construction interests with which it was allied did on the local level, it all had to do with "technical" rather than political questions.

This bureaucratic pattern contributed to the widely recognized dispersed character of the American state structure. And like the pattern of decentralization and centralization to which we referred earlier, the pattern of fragmentation was not merely random, either. Rather, fragmentation was at least in part the result of deliberate efforts to separate and insulate those government agencies that had authority over economic policies of concern to capitalists from the public world of electoral politics (see Friedland, Piven, and Alford).

IN COMBINATION, THESE various institutional arrangements created a realm of actual experience that confirmed the doctrine of separation. People saw and participated in a politics; it was a visible and a vigorous politics; and it was not a politics of property. Meanwhile, in another realm, perhaps dimly sensed but rarely seen, the politics of property unfolded. By force of law and by force of arms, that politics took its toll in the continuing expropriation and exploitation of an enfranchised people.

Of course, there was still resistance. No doctrine in a fluid and changing society can be all-embracing. People retain ideas other than those foisted upon them, and they continue to think critically about the ideas foisted upon them. The power of the doctrine of separation did not lie so much in its ability to stamp out resistance as in its ability to limit the field of battle by confining many struggles to the marketplace and by limiting the scale of those challenges to the state that occurred.

Thus the nineteenth century was marked by insurgency among working people—by zealous organizing efforts and by demonstrations, strikes, and riots. Most of these mobilizations were against employers, the direct and visible antagonists of working people, while the role of the state in maintaining domination by employers continued to be obscured. This was perhaps more the case in the large industrial cities where workers regularly gave their votes to the same machine bosses who called out the police and militia against workers in defense of property. It was perhaps less the case where machine organizations were weaker and the alliances of state and property more visible, as in the company towns of America, where workers often clearly saw and reacted to government as the enemy. Perhaps for the same reason, agrarian protests sometimes made the state the target.

Even when the state did reveal itself as the antagonist, however, it never did so among enough people at the same time. Too many people remained enmeshed in the doctrine of separation and the institutional arrangements that gave it life. Thus, at the end of the nineteenth century, when farmers in the Midwest and the South rose in protest against the banks and corporations that were destroying them, they saw the pivotal role of the state clearly. They were defeated, and defeated again and again, by the structural arrangements that made the politics of the propertied so effective. When the movement succeeded in winning state laws regulating railroad and granary rates, the corporations went to the federal courts, and the Supreme Court struck down the farmers' victories on constitutional grounds. Meanwhile, federal regulatory legislation stole the thunder of the Populist campaign against the "trusts and combinations." And when the farmers themselves turned to national politics in a campaign that culminated in the election of 1896, they were once again doubly defeated— first by the alliances with the silver lobby and the Democratic

Party into which they were forced by the exigencies of national electoral politics, and then by the far greater capacity of the men of property of the late nineteenth century to organize effectively on the national level.

Our assertion is not simply that various institutional arrangements tilted the outcome of every political contest toward property, although that is true. Rather, it is that although the Populists clearly recognized the alliance of state and property, they were ultimately unable to overcome the institutionalized advantages of the propertied because they could not mobilize support among enough other Americans who shared their understanding. The structural arrangements that enabled corporations to overturn popular victories in the states by shifting the contest to the national level were not sufficiently transparent. More than that, the Populist mobilization was further weakened by sectionalism, which bedeviled the movement from within and helped defeat it from without as the "free silver" issue came to divide the country by region rather than by class. And they were robbed of support again because the urban political machines continued to bind fast the loyalties of urban working people in the face of the Populist appeal. It is no doubt true that the champions of the silver lobby—William Jennings Bryan and his running mate the eastern financier Arthur Sewall—would have proved less than saviors had they won the election of 1896. Corporate leaders, however, were taking no chances, and mobilized for McKinley in a great frenzy by pouring unprecedented funds, organizational effort, and alarmist propaganda into the campaign. And when they did, industrial workers followed corporate money into the Republican Party.

To FOIST THE DOCTRINE of the separation of politics from economics on a people is a remarkable feat. In the United

States it was especially remarkable, for it persuaded Americans that the most pressing issues of their daily lives had nothing to do with the democratic rights for which they had fought and of which they were so proud. This extraordinary feat was not accomplished by propaganda or mere sleight of hand. It was accomplished by nothing less than the construction of a world in which the doctrine was made real, a realm of lived experience in which democratic rights mattered, but from which economic grievances against property were barred. Still, no social construction lasts forever.

4

THE
CRUMBLING
of the
WALLS

*I*T MATTERS GREATLY in history that those who are ruled can sometimes see through the ideologies promulgated by their rulers. In the twentieth century, capitalism itself contributed to the demystification of *laissez-faire* ideas, for the economy expanded and changed in ways that progressively exposed the reliance of capital on the state. Productive capacities grew, the organization of production became more concentrated, and the need for stability and growth in capital markets and consumer markets increased. As capitalism expanded and changed, so did the forms and extent of popular resistance. Taken together, these developments led to pressures for new kinds of state intervention in the economy, and thus for a greatly enlarged state role in the economy. As this happened, the institutional walls constructed around the world of popular politics began to give way, overwhelmed by the sheer scale of state action on behalf of property.

Industrialists themselves were key political actors in the process of state expansion. To cope with the instabilities entailed by growth and the popular protests that followed, they called on government for help. Thus the rapid industrial expansion of the post–Civil War period was characterized by ferocious competition and overproduction, which was ultimately moderated somewhat by the introduction in the Progressive period of a federal regulatory apparatus that worked closely with capital. But the dynamics that led to this partial solution were complicated, compounded by the pressures created by industrial anarchy and popular protest.

Within industry, competition and overproduction promoted consolidation, and the great industrial and financial empires of the late nineteenth century were the result. Railroad lines multiplied as companies jockeyed with each other in a reckless race to span the country and reap the enormous profits that control of rail transportation promised. In the process, many of the companies went bankrupt, as did other corporations as well. Competition and overproduction, together with fantastic levels of speculation, further aggravated the boom-bust pattern of the economy, so that the depth and scale of business crashes worsened as the nineteenth century wore on. But instability provided opportunities for the most powerful of the robber barons to absorb faltering companies into their expanding industrial empires. The magnates who gobbled up their competitors were developing their own solution to economic anarchy. The railroads that had been driving each other into bankruptcy were consolidated into a few huge companies, and these companies in turn were allied with steel, and steel with oil, through vast interlocking directorates. The solution to anarchy, in short, was the trust and the combination.

The "trusts and combinations" soon became anathema to the hard-pressed farmers of the Populist movement and to the allies they were able to find among industrial workers—the Knights of Labor, for example. Their movement was soon defeated. But the very stratagem used to defeat it helped initiate the process that weakened the structural foundation of the doctrine that politics had nothing to do with economics. That stratagem was to create the appearance, but not the reality, of government action against corporate excesses. As the railroad lawyer who was to become the attorney general under Cleveland explained when the first major regulatory agency, the Interstate Commerce Commission, was established in 1887, the commission "satisfied the popular clamor for a government supervision of railroads, at the same time that supervision is almost entirely nominal" (Zinn, p. 253). He was right on both counts, and legislation to regulate industry proliferated while producing little effect in curbing the activities of corporate capital. But this great parade of government measures to defend the people against property was important in another way. Again and again, as American corporate leaders conceded the legislation that would placate an inflamed public opinion, they prepared the way for the idea that government had something to do with economic life after all.

If the immediate impetus was to appease public clamor, the regulatory apparatus created during the Progressive era also suggested an additional solution to the problem of competition and overproduction. From the Interstate Commerce Commission and the Sherman Anti-Trust Act of the late nineteenth century, to the mechanisms created for the regulation of the meat-packing, rail transportation, and communications industries under Theodore Roosevelt, to the establishment of the

Federal Reserve Board and the Federal Power Commission under Wilson, the leaders of industry and finance learned, if they did not already know, the usefulness of government in ensuring a measure of stability and predictability for their ever more concentrated industrial and financial empires. When the Federal Reserve Board was created in 1920, for example, it was self-consciously intended as a mechanism to be run by bankers for bankers in order to bring stability to financial markets.

The Great Depression stimulated a new wave of demands by capital. Given the rapid advance of economic concentration, economic collapse was more widespread and its effects more pervasive than ever before. Not even the moguls of the corporate and financial worlds were spared. Within a year of the great stock market crash, their panic was evident. Bernard Baruch called for government mechanisms through which industries could eliminate "uneconomic competition." By 1931 the Chamber of Commerce and the National Association of Manufacturers called for similar measures. Agricultural, financial, and commercial interest groups added to the clamor, demanding tax abatement from local governments and a variety of government subsidies and protections on the national level. And of necessity, given the scale of the economic catastrophe and the near-helplessness of state and local governments that were themselves teetering on the brink of bankruptcy as the Depression wiped out their revenue sources, the demands that the federal government take action became insistent.

At first, the federal government resisted demands for action. But as the Depression worsened, as industrial production plummeted, and as the banking system descended into chaos, demands became more strident. In the summer of 1932, Hoover acceded to the establishment of the Reconstruction Finance Corporation that made federal loans available to private busi-

nesses and state governments. And immediately after his inau-
guration in 1933, Roosevelt pushed through the well-known
rush of legislation of the "first hundred days." The National
Industrial Recovery Act created the mechanism that industrialists had been calling for: industry-wide boards dominated by
industry representatives who would regulate production and fix
prices, with government authority. Farmers—those who
owned their land—got the Agricultural Adjustment Act, which
established price supports and cheap credit (ironically meeting
one of the demands of the Populist movement a half-century
too late, as Goodwyn points out, for many small farmers had
long since been forced off their land by indebtedness). Public
works programs were funded by the federal government on a
huge scale and were used to build the highways, airports, and
bridges needed by business and industry that the states and
localities could no longer afford to construct. A little later, in
1934, the Securities and Exchange Commission was established to stabilize financial markets. Sweeping tariffs that had
been enacted under the Hoover administration were modified
by reciprocal trade agreements to promote the sale of American goods abroad. And the Interstate Oil and Gas Compact
"fixed prices for a generation in the high-technology industries" (Ferguson and Rogers, p. 590).

Business thus continued to exert decisive influence on the
state during the Depression. But the sources of its power had
become more complex, in ways already signaled during the
Progressive period. In part, its power arose from the usual
resources of the propertied—from the fact that money, organization, media control, prestige, and social connections matter
in swaying political leaders. In part, it arose from the structural
advantages of property in American political institutions. And
paradoxically the power of business was also a reflection of the
growing power of democracy shown in the election of 1932. If

business was demanding government action in order to restore the economy, so were voters. The election gave clear evidence that voters had been activated by economic issues: formerly nonvoting members of the working class turned out in large numbers to support Roosevelt, while many other working-class voters repudiated traditional loyalties to the Republican Party. Nor was there reason to believe that these voters would become less discontented and less active so long as the economic calamity persisted. Thus the Depression not only exposed the acute dependence of concentrated capital on the state; it also revealed the political dependence of the state on capital. For, barring the kind of radical institutional transformation that politicians eschew, political stability depended on economic stability and prosperity.

Government interventions during the Great Depression did not reflect the demands of industry alone. Economic collapse stimulated massive waves of popular insurgency. The scale of these movements was made possible by increasing economic concentration that brought more and more people closer together in factories and cities where they were subjected to similar experiences. It was also made possible by the increasing scale of economic instability, which exposed so many people to the same joblessness, the same wage cuts, the same speed-ups. These movements, in other words, arose from new capacities for collective action afforded working people by the evolution of American economic development, and they were at the same time a reaction against features of that development. Moreover, the movements were shaped by political developments. On the one hand, they were still influenced by the old institutional arrangements that had segregated popular politics from the politics of property; on the other hand, they were also influenced by the escalating demands of property that were undermining these arrangements.

One form insurgency took was protest by the unemployed on a far larger scale than had ever occurred before. When factories, mines, and mills slowed to a standstill in the aftermath of the Crash, unemployment rose rapidly, affecting perhaps as much as one-third of the work force. In the industrial cities, where unemployment was concentrated, the jobless took to the streets in mob lootings, rent riots, sit-ins, demonstrations, and marches. Their demand, raised aloft on banners everywhere, was "bread or wages." Shortly afterwards, the Townsend movement's demand for pensions attracted unprecedented numbers of the aged as well as a newly awakened public sympathy for their plight. In other words, mass movements arose asserting the right to subsistence, and asserting it as a political right.

The renaissance of the idea of economic rights as political rights surely had something to do with the sheer scale of unemployment, simply because, with so many out of work, the deeply rooted *laissez-faire* idea that economic misfortune was visited only on those who lacked talent or industry could not remain so credible. And perhaps the scale of the calamity also made its objective sources in the structure of the American economy more apparent. Factories had ground to a halt; the banks had shut their doors; local governments were in chaos. There was palpable evidence in the experience of the jobless that they were in trouble because American economic institutions were in trouble, and perhaps this helped turn the private shame of unemployment into public anger and indignation.

The protests of the unemployed were more than an expression of anger over hardship and unemployment. They were also political protests in the narrow and specific sense that anger was turned against government. People had come to think that government was in some way responsible for dealing with their economic plight. And perhaps they were able to think so not only because of the extent of hardship, or the transparent fact of a system in chaos, but because the pageant of Progressive legislation that portrayed government as trustbuster and economic regulator blended images of economy and polity.

Still, in their origins, the movements of the unemployed were shaped by the institutional arrangements that had always shaped the boundaries of American popular politics. They grew in the localities because popular movements always depend on the local networks of work and neighborhood to bring people together, and in their early stages they made demands on local governments because local government in the United States had always been the main arena for the expression of popular political demands. But the scale of the movements and the nature of their demands rapidly overloaded the capacities of local governments to respond. Gosnell tells, for example, of the helplessness of the Chicago machine captains, accustomed to doling out small favors and a handshake, when they were confronted by the overwhelming volume of pleas from their stricken constituents for jobs and handouts. In city after city the breadlines grew, and local officials exerted themselves to do something even as municipal revenues were declining as a consequence of economic collapse. Local governments could not resist the economic demands of the unemployed, and because they could not respond adequately to them either, the protests could not be contained within the sphere of local politics which had successfully organized and limited democratic politics in the past. The reverberations of unrest thus spread upward, to national politics. Mayors themselves became national lobbyists for the unemployed as they sought to cope with political discontent and shrinking revenues. Increasingly, the movements directed their energies to the federal government.

The Depression also saw the rise of a mass movement among

industrial workers who made economic demands on the state. The mobilization of labor protest was due in part to industrial growth and concentration, which enlarged the numbers of industrial workers and brought them together in the mass production industries, thus enhancing their capacity for collective action and increasing the leverage they could exert on a more centralized economic structure. It was also due to the new hardships of wage cuts and speed-ups that industrialists imposed in response to falling profits and mass unemployment.

This development was long in the making. Great waves of strikes and riots had marked the late nineteenth and early twentieth centuries, for by the turn of the century industrial workers constituted 40 percent of the work force. They had cause for anger, too. One cause was wage cuts and speed-ups stimulated by competition and facilitated by the import of immigrant workers. Another was the periodic large-scale unemployment that followed each business crash. And still another was increasing mechanization and the routinization of work and degradation of skills that it fostered. The indignation of nineteenth-century workers was also incited by the emergence of corporate empires so huge and so dominant as to give the lie to *laissez-faire* notions equating the protection of property with liberty, for here was the palpable experience of the tyranny of property itself. Nevertheless, most of these great strikes were crushed. Again and again, workers demonstrated their growing capacity for economic disruption, a capacity that sprang from their larger numbers and their crucial role in the concentrated industrial economy that capital had made. And again and again, that economic power was broken by state law and state force.

What was different in the Depression was that workers also exercised effective political power, and on a national scale. They made political demands to back up their strike demands, and they made those demands of the national government. Perhaps the widespread politicization of worker discontent and its national focus owed some of its intensity to the scale and transparency of the economic disaster. Perhaps it was also a response to the background of national government regulation of the economy created during the Progressive period. And it was surely because of the fact that industrialists themselves politicized the economic crisis in a way that all could comprehend. Indeed, the National Industrial Recovery Act that industrialists wanted became the focus of indignation by workers. A clause in the act, inserted to smooth the way for the many concessions won by industrialists, granted workers the right to bargain collectively. The right was symbolic, to be sure, since there was no provision for enforcement. That clause nevertheless became the rallying point of the labor movement of the 1930s. In this particular sense, capital helped politicize the issue of worker rights in industry; it was capital that again breached the walls barring popular economic grievances from the public world of politics. And once it did, the federal government was drawn into the labor movement. The New Deal thus became as much the target of the demands of insurgent workers as industrialists themselves.

And the New Deal responded. Within weeks after Roosevelt took office, the unemployed were granted the Federal Emergency Relief Act (FERA), which moderated the impact of unemployment by putting some 20 million people on relief rolls. The first federal relief program in American history was thus launched. Two years later, with strikes spreading and the election of 1936 looming, workers won the National Labor Relations Act, which committed the federal government to protect their rights to organize and bargain collectively. At the same time, Roosevelt pressed for passage of the Social Security Act, which provided pensions for many of the old, and categorical assistance programs for others of them, as well as a categorical assistance program for families without fathers and insurance benefits for some of the unemployed. Prior to the off-term election of 1938, and in the face of another slump that threatened renewed insurgency, measures were enacted to regulate wages and hours and to authorize public housing construction to stimulate the economy and to house low-wage workers. With these measures, the framework of the contemporary social welfare state was established.

Even while these popular victories were being won, however, businessmen were mobilizing to curb or reverse them. One source of their concern, then as now, was that large-scale government relief interfered with low-wage work. As the early emergency relief program expanded, businessmen grew indignant. The legislation that followed was shaped in the vortex of the conflicting forces of popular demands and business opposition. In 1935, emergency relief was eliminated. The Social Security Act presumably took its place together with a work relief program (popularly known as "WPA"). But the work relief program petered out in a few short years, and it took time for the provisions of the Social Security Act to be implemented. The unemployment and categorical assistance provisions depended on implementation by the states, and the state legislatures moved slowly. They also legislated very low benefit levels and excluded many of the poor. Few people, for example, were admitted to the categorical assistance program for impoverished families with children (ADC, later called AFDC). And this was true despite the accelerating displacement of people from Southern agriculture during and after World War II and the relatively high levels of unemployment in the cities to which these agricultural families migrated. Public housing programs were cut back in the 1950s. And those of the old who depended solely on Social Security were kept in poverty by low benefit levels.

Business also mobilized to roll back labor's victories, and with even greater determination. The corporate counterattack began with the smashing of the "Little Steel" strike and the initiation of a red-baiting campaign in the late 1930s. The counterattack was interrupted by World War II, but the great wave of postwar strikes created a justification for its revival, this time made easier by the onset of the cold war abroad and the red scare at home. Many union leaders accommodated, and joined in the purging of the left as they turned to business unionism and the Democratic Party. The unions also lost a good deal of what they had won with the enactment of the restrictive provisions contained in the Taft-Hartley Act and, later, the Landrum-Griffin Act.

For all that ordinary people lost, they did not in fact lose everything. The gains they retained were more than skeletal. In this important respect, the men of property had been set back. People emerged from these years with a greater awareness of their economic rights as workers, as old people, as unemployed people, as poor people, in more or less that order. And they had won a framework of legislation defining some of those rights that could be drawn upon by others, at some future time.

WORLD WAR II greatly strengthened the links between government and capital because of the enormous productive demands generated by war contracts; it also enlarged the means through which state and capital together attempted economic regulation, including the wartime regulation of labor. None of this was remarkable or exceptional; wars have always been the occasion for state expansion into the economy, and World War II was merely no exception. What was significant, however, is that federal intervention continued after the war, mainly in the form of Keynesian policies to subsidize invest-

ment and maintain aggregate demand. The instruments of this
new, obvious, and full-fledged political economy included high
levels of military and defense spending that stimulated the
great boom in the Sun Belt; subsidies and tax credits for the
construction and real estate industries that helped produce the
great post–World War II suburban construction boom and the
redevelopment of the older central cities to accommodate corporate administrative functions; infrastructure subsidies in the
form of highway, water, and sewer grants that spurred the
suburbanization of housing and industry; farm subsidies that
contributed to the continuing concentration of agriculture;
and, somewhat later, the use of investment tax credits as a
strategy for economic stimulus. A number of analysts attribute
these developments to a "growth coalition" composed of political and corporate leaders (Mollenkopf; Wolfe). Corporate
leaders, however, were the dominant actors. They obtained
much more than government measures to stimulate domestic
economic growth, for the eventual benefit of both state and
property; they also obtained tax and tariff policies favorable to
American overseas investment, and used developments such as
the Bretton Woods agreement and the International Monetary Fund to facilitate overseas expansion, all of which promoted the internationalization of American capital but ultimately destabilized the domestic economy, which was not to
the benefit of the state.

These developments transformed the economy and politics.
The state's role in the economy not only expanded, but it
expanded in ways that lowered the institutional barriers that
had shielded earlier forms of intervention from public view.
During the Great Depression, business demanded and got
programs such as the National Industrial Recovery Act, which
breached constitutional prohibitions against state interference
with property, and the Supreme Court said as much. When

Roosevelt then threatened to "pack" the Court to protect the rest of the New Deal legislative program, the sanctity of the Court—its ostensible separation from politics and thus the separation from politics of constitutionally defined procedures for interpreting the Constitution—was flouted as well. Moreover, the sheer scale of the problems and the opportunities business confronted during and after World War II, and the scale of government intervention it demanded, exposed the national state as a principal as well as public actor in the American economy. Not only was the economy of the United States becoming intensely politicized, managed as it largely was by an alliance of state and capital, but at least some of the institutional arrangements that had once obscured the politics of property were crumbling. And it was business that was wielding the wrecking bar.

Once again, however, there were other hands on the wrecking bar. The end of the Depression did not signal the end of the politicization of popular economic demands. During the war, though, these demands were subdued and countered by appeals to patriotism. Immediately after the war, with strikes by industrial workers spreading once again, the federal government moved to appease the widespread fear that postwar demobilization would precipitate the high levels of unemployment that prevailed in the 1930s. The Employment Act of 1946 proclaimed that "creating and maintaining . . . useful employment opportunities" was the "continuing policy and responsibility of the Federal Government." Moreover, the act created a Council of Economic Advisors charged with the responsibility of promoting the economic stability and growth that would ensure full employment. As a practical matter, this was no guarantee of full employment, and in the succeeding decades average unemployment levels inched steadily upward, as we have already noted. It was, nevertheless, one more small step in the politicization of economic grievances.

A more significant step was taken as a result of the emergence of another insurgent movement, this time among urban blacks. Like so many people before them, blacks were being displaced from agriculture by the relentless processes of mechanization and concentration. They were able to act together in the protest movement of the 1950s and 1960s because migration and subsequent segregation had brought them together in greatly expanded ghettoes. They were able to make economic demands a political issue because the old doctrine of separation had weakened, its institutional supports broken by the combined and continuing claims of both property and democracy. And they could hope that these demands would be effective because migration to the cities had given them voting rights, and their concentration in the old industrial cities gave them power in the strongholds of the ruling Democratic administrations of the 1960s.

The black movement did not burst forth without its own distinctive history. Part of that history was formed in the South, where blacks had been tenants and sharecroppers in the semifeudal plantation system. Southern political institutions had enforced this serf-labor system by disfranchising blacks, segregating them, and subjecting them to state terror when they challenged caste boundaries. During and after the Second World War, Southern agriculture began to mechanize, so that tenantry and sharecropping gave way to wage labor. This change in itself rendered anomalous the distinctive political institutions of the caste system. But anomalous political institutions were not alone sufficient to generate protest among blacks. More important, the rural economy of the South ejected its superfluous black laborers, forcing them to migrate to the cities of the South and the North, where many were incorporated into the wage-labor system, and where they were also partially incorporated into electoral representative institutions. It was these changes that helped account for the emergence of new aspirations among blacks, and for their new capacities to act on those aspirations.

These aspirations and capacities were expressed differently in the South, where the movement began, than in the North. The Southern movement was a civil rights movement; within the caste system, blacks recapitulated the history of so many people before them and demanded political rights. In a way, this was odd. A deeply impoverished people who had been thrown off the land might have been expected to make economic demands. Instead, they fought for the desegregation of public accommodations and the right to vote. Like the mechanics and laborers of the Revolutionary period, they too believed in the promise of democracy—that political rights would yield them the power to act on their economic grievances.

The Southern movement had a large influence on the subsequent mobilization of black people in the North. Southern blacks who risked mob and police violence to challenge caste rules helped to galvanize Northern blacks by their example. And because they were largely excluded from local politics, Southern blacks chose the national government as the target of their demands from the start, thus helping to give the subsequent black movement in the North a sense of itself as a national movement, and a sense as well that its grievances belonged in national politics. Perhaps most important, the Southern movement won victories. The demands by Southern blacks for political rights captured attention and sympathy from all quarters, and forced the federal government to help break the Southern caste system.

But while Northern blacks were influenced by the example of the Southern movement and took heart from its victories, they were also influenced by distinctive experiences of their own. For one thing, they already had formal political rights, and time had showed them that political rights did not have much bearing on their poverty. More than that, the Northern movement bore the markings of the local political organizations that had always used city jobs, services, and honors to cultivate popular participation, and to organize that participation on individual, ethnic, and neighborhood bases. Although at the outset the black movement in the North demanded desegregated schools as the Southern movement had done, it also demanded better schools and a role for parents in running the schools, better neighborhood services, a share of the jobs and honors available from the municipal bureaucracies, and a share of representation in city politics, too. It did not win these things, at least not at first. It did not win them partly because intense racial animosity in the cities made it treacherous for city politicians to make concessions to blacks. And it did not win because the fragmentation and bureaucratization of city government, which had been promoted by businessmen reformers for nearly a century, had gradually diminished the control city politicians once had over much of what blacks demanded. The local apparatus of popular politics was not working, in other words, because the steadily growing black population was being excluded. And thus impeded, the Northern black movement began to escape the boundaries of local politics. More and more, the movement demanded from the national government what local governments could not or would not give. It demanded housing and income and jobs, and not just city jobs either. It demanded, in other words, subsistence rights.

The federal government responded because it was vulnerable. The Southern civil rights movement had already made it the object of black rage, and the Northern black movement

soon followed suit. Moreover, Democratic administrations of
the 1960s could not ignore intensifying conflict in the older
cities that local governments were incapable of containing, for
the New Deal realignment had made these cities the urban
strongholds of the party.

The immediate result was the battery of legislative measures
known as the Great Society. The intent was to appease the
black movement, and also to provide some of the resources that
would both push and bribe local governments to serve their
historical function of organizing popular political participation.
Although these measures provided little in the way of jobs or
income or housing, they did provide services to the insurgent
ghettoes, including information about government entitlements, legal advocates, and some organizing resources to enable the ghettoes to do battle with municipal agencies. The
federal programs also provided new funds for the municipal
agencies to smooth the way for concessions to the ghettoes.
Just as important, the Great Society generated much rhetoric
about the injustices of poverty and the state's responsibility and
commitment to do something about them. Over the next few
years these new federal resources and the heightened awareness
of federal responsibility they implied, combined with the
smoldering anger of the ghetto, created enough political pressure to force a much enlarged flow of benefits from the social
welfare programs created in the 1930s, including the programs
administered by state and local governments, and to force the
creation of new programs too. The AFDC rolls quadrupled
after 1965 and expenditures rose from $4.7 billion to $14
billion. The Medicare and Medicaid programs were enacted,
and a food stamp program was introduced that rapidly expanded to reach 20 million beneficiaries by the end of the
1970s. The elderly gained too as Social Security benefits increased sharply, partly because the black movement had politi-

cized the issue of poverty and partly because the electoral instabilities that the black movement had generated gave the votes of the aged greater leverage. Overall—after adjusting for inflation and deducting administrative costs—cash, in-kind, and service benefits rose at a rate of about 8 percent each year between 1965 and 1972. In brief, the framework of benefit programs created by the insurgent movements of the 1930s was elaborated and expanded by the insurgent movements of the 1960s.

THE MOVEMENTS OF the 1960s subsided, as had the movements of the 1930s before them. But they left in their wake a profound transformation. The movements were made possible by large changes in the American political economy and the resulting changes in popular understanding. In turn, the movements themselves confirmed and expanded those understandings. The political action of ordinary men and women had won economic victories; plain people had stayed the awesome movement of the "invisible hand." And they had engraved these victories on the legal structure of the polity through an array of laws and regulations that articulated and formalized economic rights.

In other words, the movements changed reality; they transformed the state. If the rise of popular political struggles over economic issues was made possible by the erosion of institutional arrangements that had shielded state economic activity from democratic influence, popular victories in turn created new institutional arrangements that helped expose the state to democratic influence in a continuing way. The new programs of the 1930s and the 1960s produced pervasive new linkages between the state and democratic publics that paralleled older linkages between the state and business. The structure of state bureaucracies linked to business facilitated the federal role in subsidizing investment, maintaining aggregate demand, and smoothing the way for overseas investment. The agencies established to administer the new benefit programs, services, and regulations represent another set of linkages, not with business but with the unemployed and the poor, women and blacks, the elderly and the disabled, and unions and environmental groups. By incorporating so wide a range of an enfranchised population, the state itself has become partially democratized.

On the most abstract level, these two broad sets of institutional relationships can be understood as a reflection of the interdependence of state, economy, and democracy as that interdependence took form at particular historical junctures. Relations with business reflected from the start the state's need for a stable and growing economy, both to maintain and enlarge its revenue sources and to placate powerful economic interest groups. Relations with popular groups through the benefit, service, and regulatory programs reflected not only the new demands of democratic publics but another form of state dependence that made these demands effective. The programs came into being and were expanded at moments when the state was challenged by mass protest, not in some abstract sense, but in the concrete sense that mass protest over economic issues helped to throw into jeopardy the electoral majorities on which control of the state depended.

Once created, furthermore, these programs institutionalize the interdependence of state and democracy. By responding to popular movements with national programs, the federal government has made itself the institutional locus for popular economic demands. This process began in the 1930s, but it greatly enlarged in the 1960s and 1970s. To be sure, a good many of the federal responses were in the form of grants-in-aid to states and localities that administer the programs. But the socially constructed world of local politics has nevertheless receded, overwhelmed by the scale of federal penetration of state and local government.

There is another dimension to this structural change that enlarges the vulnerability of the state to democratic influence. The social programs constitute a large and intricate apparatus of governmental and quasi-governmental organizations and personnel that is linked to and dependent on popular constituencies. This apparatus includes public agencies that administer retirement benefits, unemployment insurance, public welfare, food stamp benefits, Medicaid, Medicare, and housing subsidies. It includes the organizations that operate the job programs and job-training programs, provide counseling or rehabilitation services of one kind or another, and enforce environmental or affirmative-action regulations; and it includes the programs that reach into older and larger institutions, such as the enormous public education system, the voluntary social agencies, the hospitals, nursing homes, and other parts of the health system, and even into sectors of private enterprise such as construction, real estate, and the retail food industry. In other words, this apparatus is lodged in all levels of government, and in nongovernmental institutions as well. It is staffed by millions of people who are civil servants and social workers and construction workers and teachers and doctors and mental health workers. Furthermore, this apparatus, along with the people who staff it, is firmly linked to popular constituencies by the benefits and services provided, or by the regulations enforced, linkages that continually expose and connect it to broad groups in the population. Finally, and most fundamentally, this entire intricate apparatus with its millions of personnel exists by virtue of popular demand. It is dependent, in short, on democracy.

We recognize this sort of institutionalized interdependence

between state and society when we think about relations between government and capital. The familiar notion of the "iron triangle," for example, refers to the welding together in a pattern of mutual interdependence of the public agencies that administer business-oriented policies, the legislative committees that oversee these agencies, and the business interests that depend on agency policies. Each depends on the other, but it is business that is at the apex of the triangle, for it is business that lobbies the legislature for the increased budgets and authority that the agencies require. Now, however, this pattern of institutionalized interdependence is no longer restricted to the relations between government and capital. The benefit, service, and regulatory programs created in response to the movements of the 1930s and 1960s constitute an analogous institutionalized interdependence between state and society. These programs resulted in the establishment of a structure of agencies that is mandated to act on the rights of large population groups, that is more or less accessible to these groups, and that is ultimately dependent on them for survival. The result is not the well-organized and well-articulated interest group politics that characterizes the relations between business and government. But the result nevertheless is an institutionalized structure that tends to articulate and focus popular demands on state entities that are susceptible to these demands.

THINK OF THE DIFFERENCE. The bitter steel strikes in 1892 and 1919 were broken mainly by state militias. In 1892, the Homestead strike committee was arrested for treason. In 1919, strikers were clubbed and jailed, and immigrant workers were rounded up by the Department of Justice for deportation. But when steelworkers gathered to honor the Homestead dead in 1936, the lieutenant governor of Pennsylvania told them the steel industry was open territory for union organizers and that they could count on government to give relief benefits to strikers. Later, on Labor Day, the governor told a crowd that never during his administration would troops be used to break strikes, and "the skies returned the crowd's response" (Walsh, p. 171).

Or think of the difference between the condition of the unemployed in the late nineteenth century, when public outdoor relief was virtually abolished despite severe depressions, and their condition in the late twentieth century. When the Nixon administration announced and implemented economic policies to create the recessions of 1969–1971 and 1973–1974, it also considered it necessary to moderate the impact of these recessionary policies by allowing unemployment benefits to expand. The period of eligibility was extended to 65 weeks, and local unemployment insurance offices were kept open nights and weekends. In 1980, without any fanfare, some $26 billion was funneled through the program, up from $6.8 billion in 1972. If all this happened in the absence of widespread protest by the unemployed, it nevertheless reflected an unparalleled responsiveness by government to the unemployed, just as the steady increase throughout the 1970s in the flow of other kinds of transfer payments reflects the responsiveness by government to a variety of other beneficiary groups with which it had become linked.

America's corporate leaders have noticed these differences, too. And they have named democracy as the culprit. Leonard Silk and David Vogel attended a series of meetings of the Conference Board (a major corporate forum) in 1974 and reported that "the central tension of American capitalism, according to the common business view, is between people's rising aspirations and the inability of the American system to satisfy them without weakening its long-term viability." Businessmen are worried about being "engulfed by a rising tide of entitlement." There is "concern in the nation's boardrooms" that "democracy in America is working too well—that is the problem" (quoted in Dickson and Noble, pp. 275–6).

It is also these differences that have provoked alarm among prominent conservative European and American intellectuals. They warn of the dire consequences of the intrusion of popular economic demands into democratic politics. " 'Unrestrained appetite' has moved from the economic realm to the polity," says Daniel Bell, with the result that economic expectations have been converted "into a range of *entitlements*" (emphasis in original, p. 23). Crozier complains that European political systems are "overloaded" with participants and demands, and so the feeling spreads that democracies have become ungovernable (p. 12). Brittan offers a similar diagnosis of the British malady, where democracy is endangered by the "excessive expectations . . . generated by the democratic aspects of the system," which force politicians to incite an inherently incompetent electorate to want and demand more (p. 130). And Huntington warns of the "danger of overloading the system" in the United States as a consequence of what he calls a "dramatic renewal of the democratic spirit," expressed by the surge in participation and rising demands for equality (pp. 59 ff.).

It is not the overall politicization of the economy that concerns these intellectuals; they are preoccupied only with the intrusion of popular economic demands into political contexts. Demands for equality or for entitlements are the problem, and such demands do not emanate from the top of society. They surge from the bottom. It is not the propertied who are overloading the system. It is ordinary people who have become too clamorous, who want too much. Huntington even hints at the necessity of returning to the old solution when he warns that

"there are potentially desirable limits to the indefinite extension of political democracy" (p. 115).

What alarms these intellectuals is the revival and expansion
in a new form of the old belief that people have a political right
to subsistence. This was the belief that property tried to eradi-
cate during the centuries in which labor markets were developing. But the long historical process through which the interdependence of the state and the economy grew stronger and
became ever more apparent revived the idea that people have
a political right to a livelihood, and revived that idea in the
context of democratic rights. A people who had become incited and mobilized by that idea forced government to inaugurate and then to expand the income-maintenance programs of
the welfare state.

BUT RESOURCES FOR subsistence that do not depend on wage
labor have always obstructed efforts by employers to expand the
pool of wage labor and to intensify exploitation. Consequently,
just as employers mobilized against subsistence rights earlier in
history, so they have mobilized again.

5

DEMOCRACY
AGAINST
CAPITALISM

*A*CENTURY AND A HALF after the achievement of
formal democratic rights, the state has finally become the
main arena of class conflict. Working people who once looked
to the marketplace as the arena for action on their economic
grievances and aspirations now look more often to the state.
This ideological transformation has been so complete that economic issues now dominate electoral politics, and not only at
times of extraordinary disruption and popular mobilization.
Every presidential campaign since 1932 has featured claims
and counterclaims, promises and counterpromises, intended to
appease popular economic discontent. Unemployment has
been a key issue, a circumstance that has led political leaders
to attempt to coordinate the business cycle with the election

cycle: "Unemployment levels twelve to eighteen months before presidential elections have exceeded unemployment levels
at election time in six of the eight presidential elections" between 1948 and 1976 (Tufte, p. 19). In the 1960s and 1970s,
economic discrimination against minorities and women
emerged as a source of contention, and inflation has recently
been added to the litany of grievances.

Nor, as we have been at pains to point out, have presidents
and legislatures been able to escape the implications of campaign rhetoric once they are in office. Over the past fifty years,
programs to deal with popular economic grievances have been
initiated and then expanded. When possible, political leaders
coordinated the expansion of benefits with the election cycle:
"In four of the last seven election years, governmental transfer
payments have reached their yearly peak in October or November" (Tufte, p. 39). And in recent years, successive administrations have faltered and stumbled, paralyzed by the choices
between the tight-money/high-unemployment macroeconomic policies advocated by sectors of business and industry
and the expansionist policies demanded by working people.

The politicization of economic issues has in turn contributed
to the inability of the state to deal with the spiraling price rises
of the 1970s. A depression might indeed wring inflationary
pressures out of the economy. It might dry up excessive debt
and speculation, bankrupt inefficient firms, and drive down
labor costs. This has been a traditional "cure" for inflation in
the capitalist economy and it wreaks a bitter toll, especially
among working people. But neither business nor workers want
that cure, and no president has been free to administer it. The
result has been stalemate and stagflation.

It is a further measure of the extent to which economic
issues have become politicized that corporate mobilizations
must now be backed up with rhetoric directed mainly at the

most popular economic grievances. Big business has no votes; it cannot win elections by mobilizing in its own name or in its own interests, and it never could. Corporate victories at the polls in the past were won by mobilizing people around nationalism, nativism, racism, regionalism, and with the aid of the political machines. These themes still matter. But they are now overshadowed by straightforward economic concerns that must be addressed directly. That was certainly the case in the election of 1980: the state of the economy, which dominated the campaign debates, was not discussed from the perspective of the problem as perceived by big business, but rather in terms of the problems of unemployment and inflation, which were the relevant issues for ordinary people. As we noted at the outset, the critical defections from the Democratic ranks were concentrated among those for whom unemployment was the greatest concern. Moreover, the inability of the congressional Democrats to withstand the subsequent onslaught against the tax structure and the social program budget was itself partly a reflection of their demoralization in the wake of Carter's inability to manage the economy.

The emergence of the state as the principal arena of class conflict confronts big business with a crisis of power whose dimensions are comparable to the earlier struggle by capital to win control of the state from the alliance of monarchy and landed classes. From this perspective, the new administration's efforts to reverse the policies through which people have finally been able to compel the state to protect them in marketplace relations is only the surface manifestation of an evolving conflict of profound importance. The deeper expression of this conflict will take form over efforts to reverse the ideological and structural developments that now make the state susceptible to popular influence. Unless capital is able to restore the vitality of old doctrines, and more important, unless it is able to reconstruct the institutional arrangements that once helped sustain those doctrines, its current successes in dismantling or reducing the array of twentieth-century social programs will be short-lived. Worsening economic conditions will once again bring to power national administrations committed to acting upon popular economic grievances by rebuilding the welfare state, and even adding to its power. The critical analytical problem, then, is to evaluate the likelihood that this administration, or any future administration, can succeed in reversing the ideological and structural developments that made popular mobilizations over economic issues possible in the first place.

THE IDEOLOGICAL SIDE of the struggle is evident in the corporate campaign to revive the doctrine of the separation of the political and economic worlds by warning us of the dire consequences of "big government." These *laissez-faire* arguments about the perils of political interference in the workings of the market still retain some influence. Moreover, the arguments are being broadcast by the White House and corporate America together, and their combined voices are loud and authoritative, the more so because they evoke the nostalgic power of past beliefs. Nevertheless, the popular ideology of the twentieth century—the view that political rights are also economic rights—is by now more deeply rooted, and it has been continually confirmed by twentieth-century experience. To be sure, authoritative-sounding pronouncements made to an anxious citizenry may win a particular election. Words alone, however, have never been powerful enough to transform popular interpretations of the world in a lasting way.

The present administration is also moving to rebuild some of the institutional arrangements that once breathed life into the doctrine of separation. One way is by attempting to decentralize authority over programs inaugurated in response to popular pressures—to strengthen some of the arrangements that once restricted popular political participation and influence to the local level. Nor is this the first such attempt. The Nixon administration's revenue-sharing proposals, launched with the cry of "returning power to the people," would have accomplished the same end, because revenue sharing shifted authority for the allocation of some federal expenditures to the states and localities. But Congress balked at revenue sharing, so that only a watered-down version of the scheme was implemented. Congressional opposition might have been overcome after the landslide election of 1972 if the White House had not been discredited by the Watergate scandals.

The new administration is pursuing the same scheme, with notable determination. It too was partly thwarted in the first round of congressional action on its proposals for "block grants," with the consequence that relatively little federal authority over programs was relinquished. But the administration will try again. In its partially successful attempt to institute block grants during the spring and summer of 1981, it singled out some programs in education, health, community development, and social services. Now it is considering schemes to shift authority over the AFDC and food stamp programs to the states, and perhaps authority over Medicaid as well. These programs critically affect the lives of the very poor. Moreover, the pending proposals may be far more radical in another way. The Nixon revenue-sharing plan, and the first round of Reagan's block-grant proposals, only attempted to increase state and local authority over the allocation of federal funds. The new proposals may well go much further by coupling transfer of program authority with a shift in revenue-raising responsibility, perhaps with some federal taxes earmarked for the states and localities to ease the way.

If decentralization succeeds, the effects would be many. First and most obviously, the national organizations and national constituencies that have developed to press popular economic demands would tend to become fragmented as political energies now focused on the federal government were diffused among the states and localities. At the same time, as has already become apparent, the funding cuts that accompany decentralization intensify competition for resources among these localized fragments, further weakening their political force. Popular economic demands are thus being deflected from the national political arena and channeled into an increasingly competitive state and local politics, sparing the national government not only the reverberations of current discontent but also the reverberations of future discontent generated by the effects on working people of ongoing federal policies favorable to business interests.

If a good many popular economic grievances can be diverted into state and local politics, options for dealing with them will be greatly constricted. State and local governments have little influence over the economic conditions that generate wealth and poverty. They are also much more vulnerable than the national state to the political power that can be exerted by a mobile capital. Investors can and do bargain for favorable tax and policy concessions as the price of putting their money to work in one or another state or locality. That considerable form of pressure could well be used by investors to limit social programs so as to curb their labor-market effects.

One consequence would be to reverse the pattern, apparent since the 1930s, by which nationally administered programs created something approaching a national minimum income, and therefore a national floor under wages. Currently, the extent of state authority over benefit levels and eligibility criteria varies from program to program. Older programs, like

AFDC, give the states more authority; the result has been that the wages prevailing among the lowest-paid workers in a state or region have tended to set a ceiling above which state AFDC benefits do not rise. Moreover, certain categories of people have tended to be excluded from these programs altogether, particularly where the local economy requires large numbers of irregular or seasonal workers. However, the more recent federal income-maintenance measures, such as the food stamp and medical programs, promulgate national benefit standards and national eligibility criteria, with the consequence that these programs have tended to equalize benefits and to reach more people, thus exerting an upward pressure on local wage levels. Decentralization would remove this national equalizing effect and expose state-administered programs to the pressure of investors who can decide to go elsewhere in search of lower taxes and cheaper labor. The result, for the country generally, would be to drag benefit levels and eligibility criteria down to the levels prevailing in the low-wage states and localities. And since it would be state governments that were restricting eligibility and lowering benefit levels, the Reagan administration could avoid the onus of slashing these programs directly.

The vulnerability of state governments to investor pressure also explains why state and local patterns of taxation are so regressive, why they bear so heavily on working people. In turn, regressive tax patterns greatly aggravate hostility toward programs for low-income families that are partly financed from state and local revenue, as is evident in the antagonism directed against the AFDC and Medicaid programs, which are administered and partially financed by the states (and sometimes by counties). Consequently, the plan to localize responsibility for organizing solutions to the economic grievances of the poor would both constrict the options for dealing with those grievances and constrict the options for dealing with the political conflicts they generate. Finally, if a business-oriented national administration were to succeed in imposing these constraints, they might tend to become invisible as political issues and instead appear to be merely the boundaries of the possible, as was once the case.

Other structural reforms are being instituted within the federal government so as to make its departments and agencies less accessible to popularly based interest groups, but very accessible indeed to business groups. One such change is in the structure of representation implicit in bureaucratic appointments. Practical politics and long-honored custom have required that there be a certain match between agency appointments and the interest groups most active and influential in the policy area over which a particular federal agency presides. This practice is usually justified by the need for bureaucratic appointees to possess expertise, and in the past, this criterion justified recruitment from the business groups that had a stake in a given set of bureaucratic policies. The result was a familiar pattern that has often been commented upon: the regulatory agencies established earlier in the century came to be staffed by people recruited from the regulated industries.

This pattern was extended but also altered in the 1960s. Many new regulatory agencies were created in response to popular agitation spearheaded by civil rights, labor, environmentalist, or feminist organizations. The bureaucratic personnel for the new agencies were not drawn from industry but tended to be chosen from among these activist organizations. No longer, however. The Reagan administration has already restored the old pattern of exclusive industry representation. The high-level appointees to the Environmental Protection Agency are not environmentalists; they are lawyers from the industries affected by environmental regulations, such as Mobil and Exxon. Even the head of the Department of Labor, an appointee customarily selected because of his established links to organized labor, is now a businessman, and one hostile to organized labor at that. It is as if the new administration were trying to insulate not only parts of the federal government from the sight or sound of democratic influence but rather the whole of the federal apparatus.

Sweeping tax cuts represent the most significant structural change. A future administration will have difficulty reversing shifts in patterns of program decentralization or bureaucratic representation. The changes in the tax structure, however, will be even more difficult to reverse. The revenue-extracting capacity of the federal government was built up gradually over a long period of time. Moreover, the major increases in this power were made possible only by wartime mobilizations: the initial shift to income taxation as a major source of federal revenue took place during World War I, and the major expansion of taxing authority was made possible only by World War II. Now that so much revenue has been forfeited, it will be difficult for a future national administration to reclaim lost resources except in the event of another war, or in the event of a popular mobilization of comparable national proportions.

Of course, the mounting deficits resulting from the tax cuts and defense increases are producing second thoughts, even among Republican leaders. At this writing (November 1981), the Reagan administration's short-term economic projections have turned out to be disastrously wrong. Anticipated 1982 budget deficits may be as much as three times the projected figure of $42 billion, and equally unprecedented deficits loom for the years ahead. These future deficits, resulting from the tax cuts and rising military expenditures, will generate enormous pressure for further cuts in the programs that maintain a national income floor. Efforts to impose some new taxes are also probable. But these are likely to be regressive taxes that will hurt workers and consumers. Big business, flushed with victory, is not likely to give up what it has won through the Reagan tax cuts easily.

The structural significance of the tax cuts is that, by sharply reducing revenue, they impose limits on future government expenditures, including expenditures on social programs, and that is one intent. Thus the tax cuts narrow the parameters within which future political struggles will be fought, because the prospect of large annual deficits will make social expenditures seem impractical. Under these circumstances, fiscal austerity will not appear to be politics; it will appear to be the inevitable adaptation of a responsible government to the constraint imposed by limited resources. The tax cuts, then, are for the time being a genuine achievement for the corporate mobilization.

WHEN ITS SEVERAL PARTS are considered together, the success of the corporate campaign is impressive, at least at first glance. The groups who launched it know what they want; they are going about getting what they want forcefully and shrewdly; and they have formidable resources for propaganda and political organization, as illustrated by the stunning advertising and telephoning blitz mounted by the administration and a number of big corporations on the eve of the congressional vote on the tax-cut legislation. Their recent accomplishments are apparent. But will they succeed over the longer run? Can they revive the nineteenth-century doctrine that economic activities are regulated by the laws of the market rather than the laws of the state and thus persuade people that the state is not the proper arbiter from which to seek solutions to their economic troubles? More to the point, can they alter the structure of the state so as to make such a doctrine credible?

To ask the question in this way is to go a fair part of the way toward answering it. True, the Reagan administration is moving on both ideological and structural fronts to resurrect the old doctrine of separation. But propaganda will not alone suffice for very long; and the particular structural reforms that are being attempted are puny compared with the far larger structural changes that have accumulated to transform American society over the past century. It was these structural changes that promoted the widespread politicization of economic issues in the first place, and neither the Reagan administration nor anyone else is proposing to undo them. No one is proposing to reverse the pattern of intricate interdependency that has evolved between American capital and the state. Nor will anyone propose to do so, because this pattern was formed by developments deeply embedded in the dynamics of the capitalist economy itself. The United States has become a political economy, in the most literal and obvious meaning of the term. Neither the decentralization of a few popularly oriented programs nor the restructuring of the regulatory agencies will suffice to obscure the range of interdependencies between state and economy. Consequently, the scale and obviousness of the state's penetration of the economy will continue to nourish popular convictions that government has a great deal to do with the economic circumstances of people. It was just this "transparency of the connections between the causes and the consequences of the 'class situation'" to which Max Weber particularly attributed mass action (p. 184). If government is the connection, if it is action or inaction by government that causes declining real income or the loss of jobs, then the democratic right to participate is likely to continue to produce demands that government enact policies of economic reform.

One simple indicator will perhaps convey the extent of this transvaluation. During the Great Depression, observers reported that even while some of the jobless mobilized in righteous indignation and many others shifted uncertainly between feelings of shame and anger, most continued to feel themselves at fault. "There is in the average American a profound humbleness," Sherwood Anderson said at the time. "People seem to blame themselves" (quoted in Garraty, p. 181). But in a 1976 survey, conducted at a time when unemployment was far less severe and its institutional causes far less obvious, Schlozman and Verba found that only one-third of the unemployed believed that the jobless could find work if they just looked hard enough. From follow-up interviews designed to probe these responses, they concluded:

> [There is] little evidence that people blame themselves for their unemployed state. Their descriptions of the circumstances of job loss are quite matter-of-fact: the plant closed; business was slow; I didn't get along with my boss; I wanted to try something else; we lost a government contract. Sometimes the reports are tinged with bitterness . . . but the unemployed do not appear to hold themselves at fault. [p. 193]

This finding makes sense. It is what Garraty, in his history of unemployment, calls the internalization of the Keynsian value system: "If, in order to cool an overheated economy, a government may deliberately cause workers to lose their jobs—then those who lose their jobs are unlikely to feel either personally inadequate or the helpless victims of an inscrutable fate" (p. 251). It is important that the unemployed no longer feel so personally responsible, for part of the power of market ideology was that it turned the victims of economic hardship against themselves, and by doing so helped to make them politically impotent.

Laissez-faire slogans may still resonate, for their very familiarity gives them a nostalgic plausibility. But slogans are only slogans. The once deeply rooted belief that market forces sort out and reward the talented and industrious and punish the untalented and slothful has faded. The doleful justice meted out by the invisible hand is giving way to a struggle over the justice and injustice meted out by the state.

Measured by the standard of an intellectually developed ideology, these beliefs may seem inadequate. After all, Americans have not changed their views about capitalism and socialism, they do not generally identify with the "working class," demonstrate "class consciousness," or profess a blueprint for future reconstruction. What they do identify is the large role of the state in the economy, and the large responsibility of the state in determining their economic well-being. However much such ideas may fall short of a satisfactory and complete analysis, they nevertheless represent a profound transformation in popular understanding of the nature of the society we live in. In other words, there is a new "moral economy": it is the moral economy of the welfare state.

Indeed, the Reagan administration has tailored its rhetoric to take account of the strength of these beliefs, with the perverse result that its conduct will confirm popular convictions that the state is responsible for economic well-being. The incantations of supply-side economics notwithstanding, the administration has staked its future popular support on success in solving the problems of the American economy. The *Wall Street Journal* may evaluate success by the effects of the new policies on the money supply, or on the deficit, or on the current account. But changes in abstract indicators will not win popular support if the actual economic conditions of working people deteriorate. When the Reagan administration announced that unemployment in October 1981 had jumped to 8 percent and that the country was sliding into a recession, the director of economic surveys for the Gallup organization pointed to the danger to Reagan's popular support:

When Ronald Reagan was running for election, people believed that something had to be done. They felt we were
headed for disaster. Reagan gave them something new. A
substantial portion of the American people are still in favor
of the Administration's economic program, but people have
many reservations against it. A majority of the people believe
it is unfair, that it favors high income people over others.
[Moreover] Reagan does not have a mandate to bring about
a recession. If recession is seen as the main outcome of his
program, then attitudes will begin to shift against him very
fast. [*New York Times*, November 10, 1981, p. D2]

Of course, the American population is diverse: different
groups and classes are exposed to very different economic experiences, and have different beliefs as a consequence. Schlozman and Verba found, for example, that those who were least
well-off and in the most economically insecure situations were
most likely to support government action to end unemployment and provide for the needy, leading them to conclude that
"latent support" for government action on behalf of the poor
and unemployed "could be activated by a political leader who
would frame the issue" (p. 209). Equally interesting, they
found that support for government intervention is strongest
among black respondents, for it is blacks who express the greatest economic dissatisfaction and the strongest class consciousness. Other surveys show that blacks report consistently high
levels of political and economic discontent, and considerable
skepticism toward official explanations of government policy—
attitudes which very likely reflect a political sophistication born
of the recent black movement experience.
   Patterns of beliefs differentiated by social class, minority
status, and employment status may turn out to matter. The
Reagan social policies will undermine the economic situation

of a broad stratum of working people. But these effects will be indirect, accomplished through a chain of effects that is not perfectly obvious. The chain begins, however, with the assault on the income-maintenance programs that support the poor, the minorities, and the unemployed, and it is among them that *laissez-faire* beliefs are weakest, class consciousness highest, and skepticism toward government deepest. In other words, the politicization of economic issues is most advanced among those people who are directly affected by the budget cutbacks, and this may turn out to be another miscalculation of the Reagan administration.

The new national administration is more seriously vulnerable in that it has chosen to fight on many fronts. It has undertaken to reverse so wide a range of federal policies that opposition by an equally wide range of groups is inevitable. The significance of this aspect of the coming conflict has hardly been noticed. We know from earlier periods of great social and political upheaval that the simultaneous defection of different constituencies is always dangerous to a political regime, as the historical analyses of Moore and Skocpol show. Insurgent peasants can be repressed by force of arms, and perhaps the American poor can be too. Peasants cannot so easily be repressed when other groups also become insurgent, however, and neither are the American poor so vulnerable to repression by an administration that simultaneously and boldly antagonizes other and more influential groups.

And there is good reason to think protests will escalate on all sides. The environmental movement, for example, with its constituency among the better-off, is already openly indignant at the Reagan administration's policies. Religious, student, civil rights, and civil liberties groups are beginning to stir in opposition to Reagan's foreign and domestic policies. These groups were crucial in past movements, and they are likely to be important again, for their organizing resources and networks are formidable and their influence on public opinion considerable. Moreover, memories of the civil rights struggle and of the protests against the war in Southeast Asia are still fresh, and the participants from those movements are still very much alive.

Organized labor will be important. True, many on the left are disappointed with the past performance of a union leadership grown increasingly conservative. But conservatism was encouraged by steady economic improvement, which kept rank-and-file members relatively satisfied. That leadership is likely to be radicalized by the pressure of a rank-and-file indignant over rising unemployment, provocative anti-union federal policies, and intense corporate efforts to roll back earlier wage and workplace victories. Moreover, the unions also have a substantial stake in the social programs, for a number of these programs protect their unemployed members. Unions in the low-wage service sector also have reason to fight the effort to flood the labor market with AFDC mothers and the disabled, just as public employee unions have reason to oppose "workfare" programs.

The aged, too, are an important oppositional constituency. When Reagan successfully pressed Congress to abolish the monthly minimum Social Security payment of $122 in the summer of 1981, the organized aged protested and Congress restored it. Moreover, the aged have a stake in protecting programs other than Social Security and Medicare. The aged poor benefit from about 40 percent of Medicaid expenditures and a significant portion of housing subsidies, and almost two million receive food stamps.

There is reason to believe that women will also become a significant oppositional force. Female political values tip to the side of peace, greater equality, and economic security. Until now, women have not been free enough of men to act on those values, even at the moment of casting a secret ballot. But in the election of 1980, a gap of 8.5 percent appeared by sex, with women showing greater opposition to Reagan on matters of foreign policy, militarization, equality, and the social programs. Bella Abzug called attention to the significance of this gap, which held across class, religious, and racial lines, for the formation of a women's bloc:

Although the press made much of Reagán's having won the blue-collar vote, 50 percent of female blue-collar workers voted for Carter, and only 43 percent for Reagan. Reagan won 47 percent of the votes of male union members, but only 39 percent of unionized women's votes. Carter won 45 percent of the unionized men's votes, and 53 percent of the unionized women's votes. . . . Catholic women gave more votes to Carter than to Reagan—45 percent to 43 percent; Catholic men gave 56 percent of their votes to Reagan and only 35 percent to Carter. Of the Hispanic vote, which was skewed in Reagan's favor by male Cuban émigrés, 62 percent of the women and only 42 percent of the men voted for Carter. Among the overwhelmingly anti-Reagan black voters, women turned out in larger numbers than men.

A constituency composed of half the voters that can deliver an electoral plurality of 54 or 55 percent has enormous potential political power. And Reagan is doing much to activate women. He is heightening the threat of war, increasing inequalities, and intensifying economic insecurity, especially among women. Under these conditions, it seems probable that the women's movement, which has been faltering, will be spurred to new activism, especially if the Reagan administration accedes to the clamorous right wing and takes up the so-called "family protection" issues, including the issue of abortion. And even if the Reagan administration manages to keep these social issues in abeyance, the women's movement has been given a dramatic opportunity to broaden its base. It has so far been a modernizing and market-oriented movement, much preoccupied with expanding the opportunities of better-educated middle-class women, and as such has been damaged by its failure to reach out to poor and working-class women. Now it has the opportunity, for the Reagan attack on the social welfare programs is very much an attack on the poorer women who make up the majority of program beneficiaries.

The simultaneous provocation of a broad range of popular groups is a dangerous game for a government in another way. Mass protests are contagious, as we know from past periods of political insurgency. It is not simply that people mimic each other; it is that mobilization among some groups provokes the hopes and aspirations of other groups and shows them a way to act on those hopes. Such contagious effects are more likely at this stage in the development of American capitalism, for the underlying connections between an imperial foreign policy and a harsh domestic policy have become clearer than ever before. Economic decline in the Northeast and Midwest has made many working people aware that one source of their troubles is the flight of American capital to other regions and states as well as to other countries where labor is kept cheap by dictatorial regimes supported by gifts of American arms and the technology of repression. The very boldness of the multifaceted Reagan program casts these intertwined connections in sharp relief—connections between foreign policies and social policies, between social policies and regulatory policies, between regulatory policies and labor policies—and exposes the corporate interests that underlie them all.

We are thus being taught, if we did not already know, the

price that a military build-up exacts of our economic and social well-being, because the Reagan administration is explaining the costs to us. It is explaining, for example, that we need to cut domestic programs and risk economic instability in order to fund the military budget. And we are also being taught, if we did not already know, whose interests lie behind the multiple assault on our domestic life. We are being taught about those interests by the Reagan administration's own proclamations that increased business profits are its goal and by its frank courting of America's business elite. With these policies and postures, therefore, the Reagan administration risks not only the simultaneous provocation of a diverse range of groups, but the concomitant arousal of groups who will look upon one another as allies with a common enemy instead of as competitors, even across lines of class, race, age, and gender.

FINALLY, CAPITAL IS mobilizing against the gains made by democracy at a time when the state itself has been transformed in ways that make it far more susceptible to popular pressures. This transformation resulted from an accumulated history of democratic victories institutionalized within government. Left analysts have tended to view these victories as co-optative, as new systems of social control. They are systems of social control, to be sure. But that is not all they are. Social control is never complete, and never enduring. The very mechanisms that effect such control at one historical moment generate the possibilities for political mobilization at another. If that were not true, the history of insurgency from below would have ended long ago.

The contemporary social welfare state affords new opportunities for mobilization. There now exists an enormous array of agencies and programs oriented to popular grievances. Of course, the Reagan administration is reducing budgets and even abolishing some programs. It is also firing some of the federal civil servants who staff such programs, and no doubt intimidating a good many others into silence. But for all of its zeal, it cannot simply eliminate the huge and intricate state apparatus created in response to a history of popular demands. Nor can that apparatus be effectively disciplined either, for much of it lies beyond federal reach. The historical pattern of decentralization thus has an ironic contemporary significance, for it resulted in many popularly oriented programs being lodged in state and local government, and in private institutions that receive government contracts or are reimbursed by government for services provided. This large and intricate apparatus, together with the millions who staff it, is beyond the reach of the federal government. It stands as a source of internal bureaucratic opposition.

These state and local agencies and their staffs will be seriously affected by the budget cutbacks and the new federal constraints. Moreover, the prospect of larger and larger cutbacks means that more and more of these workers will lose their jobs, and that will become a cause for opposition. Their opposition can assume enormous importance because they are directly linked to the far greater numbers of people who will lose benefits or services or regulatory protections. The millions of teachers and health workers and social workers and state and county and municipal civil servants all interact with tens of millions of parents and patients, clients and citizens. In the past these interactions have often been hostile and antagonistic, for agency personnel were inevitably targets of much popular discontent. Now, however, the Reagan administration has set the stage for these groups to make common cause. Not only are the agencies and their personnel a natural and far-flung network for organizing, but these personnel, together with their tens of millions of citizen clients, constitute a veritable electoral host. Or, as O'Connor put the same point: "The social democracy built into the . . . bureaucratic structure is perhaps the main domestic problem facing big capital" (1981, p. 54).

Under these circumstances, federalism itself will be turned against the national administration. Governors, county supervisors, and mayors attempting to cope with the explosive pressures generated by the new federal policies will try to deflect popular anger upward. That was their strategy during earlier periods of popular insurgency: the United States Conference of Mayors, for example, was formed in the early 1930s to demand federal help in dealing with a turbulent unemployed, and in the 1960s it was again a vehicle for pressure on the federal government to respond to urban unrest. When political leaders thus lend their prestige to the legitimation of popular grievances, as Tocqueville and others have long since instructed us, the climate of denunciation becomes far more intense. In eighteenth-century France, it was mainly the *philosophes* who denounced the regime for its oppression of the people. In late-twentieth-century America, the *philosophes* will be joined by a federalism divided against itself.

EVEN WITH WIDESPREAD opposition to the Reagan program, victories are not likely to be quick and easy, for the administration and its business allies are formidable and determined, and they have already entrenched their interests in the federal budget through huge tax cuts. The threat of defeat at the polls will matter greatly; in fact it is critical. But the processes through which the electoral threat can be made effective are more complex than they appear at first glance. No mere tallying of public opinion will be enough, for public opinion needs articulated outrage and articulated alternatives to assume a clear form, and the advantages of the uses of propaganda are with the administration. The political parties themselves have become propaganda machines, more completely than ever before. The party infrastructures that once reached into the neighborhoods and towns have withered. Instead, congeries of shifting moneyed cliques compete for control of the parties in vast and sophisticated advertising campaigns. One such clique now rules the country.

But democratic influence was never realized only by taking opinion surveys or counting votes, for the decisive advantages of control of communications networks, and of the resources for the manipulation, co-optation, and coercion of public opinion were always at the behest of the moneyed interests. Those advantages could never be matched by people who confined themselves to the normal routes of persuasion and electioneering. They were sometimes more than matched when people took to the streets, or walked off their jobs, or occupied the waiting rooms of the schools or the factories. The advantages of the propaganda machines were sometimes overcome, in short, by mass protest. When people defied the rules of everyday life, when they stopped the machines or stopped traffic, the disruptions they caused articulated their outrage, made visible the demand for new alternatives, and sometimes mobilized a sufficient following to jeopardize the electoral success of political leaders who failed to respond. The electoral threat, in short, has always been activated and organized by movements of mass protest, and it is about to be again.

IF DEMOCRACY CAN no longer be contained, and if it cannot be stamped out either, then we are at a historic turning point in the development of American institutions. The point to which we have come is historic because democracy has indeed generated very large problems for capitalism. These are not the simple problems of big government, for capital itself requires a large and intrusive state. Rather, the problems developed because some of the activities of an enlarged state were shaped in response to popular economic grievances. Now, as in the past, popular economic grievances are grievances against property, and responses to those grievances have required intrusions on property.

In this sense, the "crisis of democracy" theorists have discovered an authentic crisis, although they have failed to identify its sources correctly. Their complaint is that people want more and expect more, with the result that democracies have supposedly become ungovernable. This neutral generality suggests that democratic demands exceed the limits of what is materially possible. However, it is capitalism rather than democracy that has become ungovernable, for it is capitalism that has responded to democratic demands on the one hand, and contracted economic horizons on the other, with anarchic disinvestment and speculation.

At the same time, and just as in earlier periods of contraction and uncertainty, capital is trying to maintain profits by reducing the living standards and increasing the labor effort of working people. The seriousness of this effort by corporate America to rid itself of environmental, health and safety, and affirmative-action regulatory controls does not reflect animus toward big government as such; it reflects the extent to which these controls have intruded upon and constrained the dynamics of capitalist production and profitability. And the seriousness of the corporate effort to reduce the income-maintenance programs reflects the extent to which these policies, by protecting the subsistence of working people, intrude upon and constrain the dynamics of the labor market. By acting to assuage popular economic grievances, the state has weakened the market power of capital. In other words, democracy has expanded to curb the depredations of capital. That, in the end, is what all the shouting is about, and it is indeed something to shout about.

Capital's efforts to escape the double fetters of democratic demands and contracting horizons are limited by the ultimate instability of speculative gains and by the narrowing of international markets for investment. The Third World is increasingly turbulent and precarious. Nor does it do much good to escape to the Western European markets that American capital has until now favored. The major industrial nations of Western Europe have parallel social welfare programs with parallel effects on labor-market relations, and there is no reason to expect that Western European governments will attempt the scale of cutbacks undertaken by the Reagan administration. On the contrary, there are as many signs that social democracy is gaining ground in Europe as signs that it is losing ground.

It may be that the "authoritarian" regimes favored by the Reagan administration's foreign policy will provide a safe haven for some American investment abroad. But this solution is hardly adequate to the scale of the problem confronting capital. First, there are limits to the amount of capital that can be absorbed by a shrinking number of friendly Third World dictatorships. Second, the safety provided by these countries is only illusory, for their use of force and terror cannot make these regimes permanently stable. Third, the investment by capital in domestic plant and natural resources is huge and is not likely to be abandoned; the big corporations can, in effect, be held hostage by the immobility of most of their capital. Fourth, access to our domestic markets remains a prize that even mobile capital cannot simply forfeit or ignore.

Just because its escape routes are both narrow and narrowing, capital has mobilized to reverse the intrusions of democratic politics in the United States. All of our analysis leads to the conclusion that we have reached a stage in our political development when it is possible to defeat this mobilization. If it is defeated, serious problems in the American political economy will remain to be solved, not by curtailing democratic demands, but by expanding them.

At first, the expansion of democracy forced the state to inaugurate programs that protected the poor, the unemployed, the disabled, and the aged from the vicissitudes of the labor market. These protections not only shielded the weakest groups from unemployment and hunger but, by shielding them, strengthened the bargaining power of a much broader stratum of working people. Later, democratic demands led to public measures curbing the powers of capitalists over production decisions by requiring them to take some account of the effects on the health and safety of workers and on the general environment. And the rights of employers to hire, promote, and fire at will, which were first modified by organized labor, have been limited still further by recent affirmative-action victories. The necessary next step to overcome stalemate and stagflation is to limit capital's right to invest as it chooses, especially by blocking its escape routes from democratic challenges into speculation and international markets.

ALTHOUGH THE CORPORATE mobilization in our time is formidable, its success depends finally on the inability of the American people in the twentieth century to see through the mystifications of propaganda drawn from the nineteenth century. Its success also depends ultimately on the acquiescence of Americans before the combined power of state and capital. Both premises have proved wrong before.

That these premises proved wrong before, and are likely to

prove wrong again, is due to the very success with which capitalism transformed the fatalistic outlooks and adaptations that prevailed in the traditional community. Before capitalism, Time and God combined to make people accept the world as they found it, so long as subsistence rights were respected. But capitalism destroyed subsistence rights and fractured the traditional community. In doing so, however, it challenged, undermined, and finally destroyed the authority of tradition in every sphere of life. More than that, it transformed the world, and continued everywhere and in every way to transform the world by breathtaking innovation and expansion. Capitalism thus showed by its achievements that human action matters, that authority can be defied, and that people can mobilize to remake the world. In these ways, capitalism helped give rise to political activism, and to an activist and participatory political ideology called democracy.

For a very long time, the popular aspirations and activism unleashed by capitalism were frustrated. They were frustrated by a doctrine that prescribed the separation of the political and economic spheres, and by the institutional arrangements that made the separation seem natural. Taken together, these social constructions shielded capitalism from the aspirations and activism it had unleashed. Now those defenses lie in ruins, and the possibilities of democracy remain to unfold.

Cited References

Abzug, Bella. "Forming a Real Women's Bloc." *The Nation,* November 28, 1981.

Aronowitz, Stanley. *False Promises: The Shaping of American Working Class Consciousness.* New York: McGraw-Hill Book Co., 1973.

Beard, Charles A. *An Economic Interpretation of the Constitution of the United States.* New York: Free Press Paperback, 1965.

Bell, Daniel. *Cultural Contradictions of Capitalism.* New York: Basic Books/Harper Colophon Books, 1978.

Bendix, Reinhard. *Nation Building and Citizenship.* New York: John Wiley & Sons, 1964.

Block, Fred. "Beyond Relative Autonomy: State Managers as Historical Subject." Unpublished manuscript.

Bosworth, Barry. "Re-establishing an Economic Consensus: An Impossible Agenda?" *Daedalus* 109, no. 3 (Summer 1980): 59–70.

Bowles, Samuel, and Herbert Gintis. "The Crisis of Liberal Capitalism: The Case of the United States." Unpublished manuscript.

Brittan, Samuel. "The Economic Contradictions of Democracy." *British Journal of Political Science* 5 (1975):129–59.

Burnham, Walter Dean. "The 1980 Earthquake: Realignment, Reaction, or What?" In Thomas Ferguson and Joel Rogers, eds., *The Hidden Election: Politics and Economics in the 1980 Presidential Campaign,* pp. 98–140. New York: Pantheon Books, 1981.

Castells, Manuel. *The Urban Question.* London: Edward Arnold, 1977.

Chambliss, William J. "A Sociological Analysis of the Law of Vagrancy," *Social Problems* 12, no. 1 (Summer 1964): 67–77.

Crozier, Michael. "Chapter II—Western Europe." In Michael Crozier, Samuel P. Huntington, and Joji Watanuki, *The Crisis of*

Democracy: Report on the Governability of Democracies to the Trilateral Commission, pp. 11–58. New York: New York University Press, 1975.

Danziger, Sheldon, Robert Haveman, and Robert Plotnick. "How Income Transfer Programs Affect Work, Savings, and the Income Distribution: A Critical Review." *Journal of Economic Literature* 19 (September 1981): 975–1028.

Dickson, David, and David Noble. "By Force of Reason: The Politics of Science and Technology Policy." In Thomas Ferguson and Joel Rogers, eds., *The Hidden Election: Politics and Economics in the 1980 Presidential Campaign,* pp. 260–312. New York: Pantheon Books, 1981.

DuBoff, Richard B. "Full Employment: The History of a Receding Target." *Politics and Society* 7, no. 1 (1977): 2–25.

Durkheim, Emile. *Suicide.* New York: Free Press, 1951.

Fabricant, Solomon. "The Problem of Controlling Inflation." In C. Lowell Harriss, ed., *Inflation: Long-term Problems. Proceedings of the Academy of Political Science* 31, no. 4 (1975): 156–68.

Ferguson, Thomas, and Joel Rogers. "How Business Saved the New Deal." *The Nation,* December 8, 1979.

Fiedler, Edgar R. "Economic Policies to Control Stagflation." In C. Lowell Harriss, ed., *Inflation: Long-term Problems. Proceedings of the Academy of Political Science* 31, no. 4 (1975): 169–78.

————. "Inflation and Economic Policy." In Clarence C. Walton, ed., *Inflation and National Survival. Proceedings of the Academy of Political Science* 33, no. 3 (1979): 113–31.

Friedland, Roger, Frances Fox Piven, and Robert R. Alford. "Political Conflict, Urban Structure, and the Fiscal Crisis." *International Journal of Urban and Regional Research* 1, no. 3 (1977): 447–71.

Garrity, John A. *Unemployment in History.* New York: Harper & Row, 1978.

Gilder, George. *Wealth and Poverty.* New York: Basic Books, 1981.

Ginzberg, Eli, and George J. Vojta. "The Service Sector of the U.S. Economy." *Scientific American* 244, no. 3 (March 1981).

Goodwyn, Lawrence. *Democratic Promise: The Populist Movement in America.* New York: Oxford University Press, 1976.

Gosnell, Harold F. *Machine Politics: Chicago Model.* Chicago: University of Chicago Press, 1937.

Gough, Ian. *The Political Economy of the Welfare State.* London: Macmillan Press, Ltd., 1979.

Greenstone, J. David. "Ethnicity, Class, and Discontent." *Ethnicity* 2 (March 1974).

Greider, William. "The Education of David Stockman." *Atlantic Monthly,* December 1981.

Gutman, Herbert G. "Work, Culture and Society in Industrializing America." *American Historical Review* 78 (June 1973).

Haveman, Robert H. "Unemployment in Western Europe and the United States: A Problem of Demand, Structure, or Measurement." *American Economic Review* 68, no. 2 (1978): 44–50.

Hibbs, Douglas A. "Political Parties and Macroeconomic Policy." *American Political Science Review* 71, no. 4 (December 1977): 1467–87.

Hobsbawm, E. J. *Primitive Rebels: Studies in Archaic Forms of Social Movement in the 19th and 20th Centuries.* New York: W. W. Norton & Co., Norton Library, 1965.

——. *Bandits.* New York: Pantheon Books, 1981.

Huntington, Samuel P. "Chapter III—The United States." In Michael Crozier, Samuel P. Huntington, and Joji Watanuki, *The Crisis of Democracy: Report on the Governability of Democracies to the Trilateral Commission,* pp. 50–118. New York: New York University Press, 1975.

Katznelson, Ira. *City Trenches: Urban Politics and the Patterning of Class in the United States.* New York: Pantheon Books, 1981.

Kolko, Gabriel. *The Triumph of Conservatism.* New York: Free Press, 1977.

Lubove, Roy. *The Struggle for Social Security: 1900–1935.* Cambridge, Mass.: Harvard University Press, 1968.

Marshall, T. H. *Class, Citizenship, and Social Development.* New York: Doubleday & Co., 1964.

Miller, S. M., and Donald Tomaskovic-Devey. *The Recapitalization of Capitalism,* chap. 6, forthcoming.

——, Barbara Tomaskovic-Devey, and Donald Tomaskovic-Devey. "Neo-Marxists and the Welfare State." Unpublished manuscript.

Mollenkopf, James H. "The Post-war Politics of Urban Development." *Politics and Society* 5, no. 3 (1975): 247–96.

Moore, Barrington, Jr. *Social Origins of Dictatorship and Democracy: Lord and Peasant in the Making of the Modern World.* Boston: Beacon Press, 1966.

O'Connor, James. *The Fiscal Crisis of the State.* New York: St. Martin's Press, 1973.

———. "The Fiscal Crisis of the State Revisited: A Look at Economic Crisis and Reagan's Budget Policy." *Kapitalistate* 9 (1981): 41–62.

Parsons, Talcott. *The Social System.* New York: Free Press, 1951.

Phillips, A. W. "The Relation between Unemployment and the Rate of Change of Money Wage Rates in the United Kingdom, 1861–1957." *Economica* 25 (1958): 283–99.

Piven, Frances Fox, and Richard A. Cloward. *Regulating the Poor.* New York: Pantheon Books, 1971.

———. *Poor People's Movements.* New York: Pantheon Books, 1977.

———. "The Politics of Unemployment in the 1980s." Paper prepared for the Institute of Policy Studies, Washington, D.C., 1979, unpublished.

Piven, Frances Fox, and Roger Friedland. "Public Choice and Private Power: The Origins of the Urban Fiscal Crisis." Unpublished manuscript.

Polanyi, Karl. *The Great Transformation.* Boston: Beacon Press, 1957.

Rothschild, Emma. "Reagan and the Real America." *New York Review of Books,* February 5, 1981.

Schlozman, Kay Lehman, and Sidney Verba. *Injury to Insult: Unemployment, Class, and Political Response.* Cambridge, Mass.: Harvard University Press, 1979.

Schor, Juliet B. "The Citizen's Wage: An Analysis of the Influence of Social Welfare Expenditures on the Wage Inflation–Unemployment Tradeoff." Unpublished manuscript.

Schumpeter, Joseph A. *Capitalism, Socialism and Democracy.* 3rd ed. New York: Harper & Row, Harper Colophon Books, 1975.

———. "The Crisis of the Tax State." *International Economic Papers,* no. 4, pp. 5–38. New York: Macmillan Co., 1954.

Scott, James C. *The Moral Economy of the Peasant: Rebellion and*

Subsistence in Southeast Asia. New Haven, Conn.: Yale University Press, 1976.

Skocpol, Theda. *States and Social Revolutions.* Cambridge: Cambridge University Press, 1979.

Smelser, Neil J. *Social Change in the Industrial Revolution.* Chicago: University of Chicago Press, 1959.

Thompson, E. P. *The Making of the English Working Class.* New York: Vintage Books, 1963.

———. "The Moral Economy of the English Crowd in the Eighteenth Century." *Past and Present,* no. 50 (February 1971), pp. 76–136.

Thurow, Lester. "How to Wreck the Economy." *New York Review of Books,* May 14, 1981.

Tilly, Charles. *From Mobilization to Revolution.* Reading, Mass.: Addison-Wesley Publishing Co., 1978.

Tocqueville, Alexis de. *L'ancien régime.* Trans. M. W. Patterson. Oxford: Basil Blackwell, 1947.

Tufte, Edward R. *Political Control of the Economy.* Princeton, N.J.: Princeton University Press, 1978.

Vogel, David. "Business's 'New Class' Struggle." *The Nation,* December 15, 1979.

Walsh, J. Raymond. *CIO: Industrial Unionism in Action.* New York: W. W. Norton & Co., 1937.

Weber, Max. *Essays in Sociology.* Trans., ed., and with an introduction by H. H. Gerth and C. Wright Mills. New York: Oxford University Press, 1946.

Wolfe, Alan. *America's Impasse: The Rise and Fall of the Politics of Growth.* New York: Pantheon Books, 1981.

Wolin, Sheldon S. "Why Democracy?" *Democracy,* January 1981, pp. 3–5.

Zinn, Howard. *A People's History of the United States.* New York: Harper & Row, 1980.

Index

ABOUT THE AUTHORS

FRANCES FOX PIVEN and RICHARD A. CLOWARD are the co-authors of the widely acclaimed *Regulating the Poor* (C. Wright Mills Award of the Society for the Study of Social Problems, 1971), *The Politics of Turmoil*, and *Poor People's Movements*, all published by Pantheon. They have both written extensively for political journals and national newspapers and magazines.

Dr. Piven is currently professor of political science at Boston University and past president of the Society for the Study of Social Problems.

Dr. Cloward is professor of social work at Columbia University and author of *Social Perspectives on Behavior*, and *Delinquency and Opportunity* (Dennis Carroll Award of the International Society of Criminology, 1965).